W9-BOB-624

PUSH BACK THE

by Bob Burke
with David A. Womack

DARKNESS

The Story of Don Stamps and The Full Life Study Bible

life
PUBLISHERS INTERNATIONAL

Push Back the Darkness

The Story of Don Stamps and The Full Life Study Bible

Second Edition Copyright © 2000 by
Life Publishers International
1400 N. Campbell
Springfield, MO 65802-1818

Copyright © 1995 by
Lumina Press
P O Box 4649
Springfield, MO 65808-4649

By Bob Burke
Edited by David A. Womack and Dr. Stanley M. Horton ThD.
Cover Redesigned by Gryphix
— Original Design by 2W Design Group

All rights reserved. No part of this publication may be reproduced, stored in a retrieval system, or transmitted, in any form by any means, electronic, mechanical, photocopying, recording or otherwise, without prior written permission from Life Publishers International.

Library of Congress Catalog Card Number 95-079678
ISBN # 0-7361-0168-3

Printed in the United States of America

— *Table of Contents* —

—*Foreword*—

What a joy it is to see the story of a great missionary vision. God's servant in this biography is Missionary Don Stamps, who saw a great need and simply determined that with God's help he would dedicate whatever it took to meet that need. That is servanthood with a vision!

The Stamps family—Don and Linda, with their children, Toby, Todd, and Tiffany—were Assemblies of God missionaries in Brazil. As soon as language study was finished, Don began to travel in itinerant ministry among the churches. He discovered immediately that thousands of Brazilian pastors had almost nothing in the way of personal libraries. He concluded that those pastors could be greatly assisted if they had a study Bible with Pentecostal notes. Once he knew what the need was, he proceeded to meet that need.

Nearly a decade later, that dream was accomplished. Don's clear goal and blessed persistence made the dream come true.

My life has been forever enriched by my close association with Don Stamps, a man of God with a holy and burning passion to make God's Word studied and understood.

The pages of this story will display faith in action. Don's plea was always that only God would be glorified. Here is the story of a man who lived and worked to that end.

Loren O. Triplett
Executive Director
The Assemblies of God Division of Foreign Missions

— Preface —

Don Stamps was my hero—not just because he was a great scholar and missionary, but because he was unquestionably loyal to the Bible.

Don believed—and lived—every word in the Bible. His creed was "God's Word is my final authority." Every time he faced a crisis in his life, he turned to God's Word for direction.

The idea to write Don's story came to me during his funeral service in 1991. For the next three years, I worked closely with his family and friends to glean a mountain of information about his action-packed life.

I could not have completed this task without splendid cooperation from Don's widow and children, Linda, Toby, Todd, and Tiffany Stamps; Don's parents, Woody and Emma Stamps; my able research assistants, Eric Dabney and Cindy Wilson; my manuscript editors, Dr. Stanley Horton, Rev. Ron McCaslin, Terry Davidson, Ryan Wilson, Jim and Faye Bertelmann; and Sandi Welch who designed both the cover and inside of the book.

Two of Don's closest friends, Wesley Adams and the late Jim Dimick, provided keen insight into Don's soul. Wesley worked with me closely in developing ideas into stories and stories into a manuscript.

Special thanks are due David A. Womack, manager of Ministry Resources Development for Gospel Publishing House, who did much to put the book in its final form.

Preface

The story of Don Stamps and *The Full Life Study Bible* will make you laugh—and cry—and will confirm the words of the old hymn "Great Is Thy Faithfulness."

Unless otherwise stated, Bible quotations in this book are from the New American Standard Bible (NASB),[1] which was the version Don Stamps used in writing his study notes. The decision to make the notes available in the New International Version (NIV) and the King James Version (KJV) came about in negotiations between the Assemblies of God (Life Publishers International and Gospel Publishing House) and Zondervan Publishing House. A special printing of the Bible with Assemblies of God identification in NIV or KJV is available from Gospel Publishing House.

Bob Burke
1995

1. New American Standard Bible, (Cambridge: Cambridge University Press), The Lockman Foundation, La Habra, California, 1977.

PUSH BACK THE DARKNESS

❧ *Chapter 1* ❧

Brazil in Darkness

*I*t was still dark at Campinas, and the rain was coming down in sheets as if thrown by some great bucket as Don and Linda Stamps began the three-hour drive across central Brazil to "Pinda." Nobody called it Pindamonhangaba, not even in Portuguese. For Don's American ears it sounded too much like Pandemonium—the poet John Milton's name for the place of all demons in *Paradise Lost*. This was supposed to be a tropical paradise; but there were devils, and he'd had his share of pushing back the darkness, much like his headlights were now penetrating the night. He loved Brazil and its ever-present millions of intense people; but the darkness of its spiritism was all around him, and the drums were always there, even when he could not hear them.

Campinas was northwest of Sao Paulo, and Pindamonhangaba was in the hilly coffee country on the road southeast toward Rio de Janeiro. They made this trip once a week from Campinas, where many of the missionaries lived, to Pinda, where they taught the Brazilian Christian workers in the Assemblies of God Bible school founded by John and Dorris Lemos. It was a winding, two-lane road through the Brazilian hills; and it was packed with produce trucks.

Don missed the good old winters back in Kansas—real winters with cold and snow and icicles on the farmhouse eaves. He had written to his good friend, Bob Silkman, "Linda and the kids and I get homesick when we make tapes to send you. Sure miss our days together talking over cups of coffee at

Ray's Cafe. I'd love to go to Louie's Pizza Place right now and have a pizza with you. I'd even like to load up some hay out at your farm. I miss those good cold winter days."[1]

Yes, it was easy to think of western Kansas this far away in the tropical Brazilian night; but Don and Linda knew without any shadow of a doubt that God had brought them to this mission field—perhaps for what they might do for God as missionaries, but certainly for what their experiences in this spiritual darkness would accomplish to expose the world to God's light. That was their passion, the driving force of their lives—to share with the people in the darkness the light of God's Word.

AN IDEA IS BORN

Don C. Stamps, destined to become the author of the study notes and articles in The Full Life Study Bible,[2] had come a long way since he first responded to God's call to Brazil. He had found the spiritual darkness oppressive. But there was another need that kept him awake nights and eventually brought him to the great accomplishment of his life's work. The Assemblies of God was by far the largest evangelical church in Brazil. Congregations numbered in the thousands. No new cities or towns were left to enter. Yet, there was a terrible weakness that threatened to limit the effectiveness of the Brazilian church—the lack of good Bible study materials to give depth to the Pentecostal revival.

As Don visited the churches of Brazil, he saw the urgent need of providing both training and Bible study materials for the pastors. The need was great both in rural areas where pastors rode bicycles to evangelize out-of-the-way places and in the urban, better-educated regions where so few Bible materials were available in Portuguese.

THE HOLY SPIRIT: UNCONFINED

Don began to write his Bible notes in 1982, at first to meet the spiritual needs in Brazil. Only later did he and others who encouraged him see that his inspiration would bless the whole world. Eight years later, he wrote in the Author's Preface to *The Full Life Study Bible: An International Study Bible For Pentecostal And Charismatic Christians:*[3]

"The vision, call and urgency from God for this study Bible came to me while serving as a missionary in Brazil. I realized how much Christian workers needed a Bible that would give them direction in their thinking and preaching. Thus, seven years ago I began writing the notes and articles for this work. Later, when I came back to the United States for a short period of time, I discovered a similar desire among both pastors and lay people for a study Bible with notes that have a Pentecostal emphasis."

Himself a transfer to the Assemblies of God from another denomination after being baptized in the Holy Spirit and speaking in other tongues, Don had a burden to make the Pentecostal understanding of the Scriptures clear to everyone. He was particularly concerned about the deadly doctrine of cessationism that thought that miracles of healing and deliverance ceased after the completion of the New Testament canon and therefore are not for today. Don wrote:

"During the past number of years I have written with an increasing assurance that the Holy Spirit is not confined to the pages of Scripture, but that He wants to act today as He did in Bible times. The Spirit has come to remain personally with God's people, and His abiding presence is to be manifested in righteousness and power (Mt 6:33; Ro 4:17; 1Co 2:4; 4:20; Heb 1:8). In and through the church, God's Spirit desires to work in the same manner as He did in the earthly ministry of Jesus and continued to do in the apostolic church of the first century."

In that statement, Don had captured the very heart of the Pentecostal Movement as a revival of apostolic, New Testament experience and doctrine. People who share that straightforward expectation of New Testament results in today's church needed the interpretation and inspiration of Don Stamps to put the Movement in perspective and provide a study Bible for Pentecostal and Charismatic Christians.

Don said that *The Full Life Study Bible* was founded on three fundamental convictions. First, he said:

"The original revelation of Christ and the apostles as recorded in the NT is fully inspired by the Holy Spirit; along with the OT, it is God's inerrant and infallible truth and the ultimate authority for the church of Christ today. All believers throughout history are dependent on the words and teachings of Biblical revelation for determining God's standard of truth and practice."

There he has stated the Pentecostal position that the New Testament church is the continuing pattern by which all churches must measure their Christianity.

Second, he said:

"It is the task of every generation of believers not only to accept the NT as God's inspired Word, but also to sincerely seek to reproduce in their personal lives and congregations the same faith, devotion and power demonstrated in and through the faithful members of the early church. I am persuaded that the full life in the Spirit as promised by Christ and experienced

16

by NT believers is still available for God's people today (Jn 10:10; 17:20; Ac 2:38-39; Eph 3:20-21; 4:11-13)."

This conviction that original Christianity is true Christianity had brought him through a pilgrimage from early days of youthful rebellion and through a long process of Christian development to personal obedience as a devoted servant of Jesus Christ. It was a long journey from growing up in Oklahoma to ministerial preparation and foreign missionary service. Because Don was filled with the Holy Spirit and spoke in tongues as the first believers did in Acts 2:4, he and Linda were cast from their first denomination and later joined the Pentecostal Movement. Finally, he became an outstanding spokesman of the faith for all Pentecostal and Charismatic people.

He continued with his third conviction, saying:

"The church will fully experience the original Kingdom power and life in the Holy Spirit only as it seeks with all its heart the righteousness and holiness set forth by God in the NT as His standard and will for all believers (2Co 6:14-18). Kingdom power and Kingdom righteousness go together; they cannot be separated. Jesus states that we must seek both God's 'kingdom and his righteousness' (Mt 6:33). The apostle Paul states that God's kingdom consists of both 'power' (1Co 4:20) and 'righteousness' (Ro 14:17). Thus the way to the fullness of God's kingdom with all its redemptive power is found in sincere faith in and devotion to the Lord Jesus Christ and in a separation from all unrighteousness that offends both God and the Holy Spirit whom He has poured out (Ac 2:17, 38-40)."

He summarized *The Full Life Study Bible* by saying, "The major purpose of this study Bible is to lead you, the reader, to a deeper faith in the NT's apostolic message and to a greater expectancy for a NT experience made possible by the fullness of Christ living in the church (Eph 4:13) and by the fullness of the Holy Spirit living in the believer (Ac 2:4; 4:31)."

Don Stamps set before us all a high standard of faith in original Christianity, not only for what it represents from biblical times but for the church today. It seems such a loss that he left us just before his fifty-third birthday; for it was practically with his dying breaths that he finished his final notes, closed his work, and went home to be with his Lord.

Since his passing, his widow Linda Stamps has traveled extensively to speak in churches, colleges, conferences, and church councils, presenting *The Full Life Study Bible* and giving her personal testimony of God's grace.

DARKNESS TO LIGHT

Don Stamps' life is a source of such outstanding inspiration that in the midst of our marveling at his high pinnacles of righteousness and of listening to the voice of God, we must in all fairness to future heroes of the faith point out that those were not always the characteristics by which he was known. As with all His great ones, God took an ordinary and even delinquent boy and developed him by His Holy Spirit into the man who would bless the nations with his inspired Bible notes.

This is the story of a man who came from darkness to light, conquered that darkness, and shed forth the light of God's Word for all of us. We may see him now as he sat at his arrangement of tables with his books spread out before him and wrote his notes with a black ballpoint pen on a yellow legal pad....

PUSH BACK THE
DARKNESS

∽ *Chapter 2* ∾

An Unlikely
Future
Missionary

*D*on Stamps was destined to be a preacher, but no one would have suspected it in his early years. In his bloodline on his mother's side of the family, he descended from John Knox, who led the Protestant Reformation in Scotland.

Knox was a fiery preacher who molded the Church of Scotland during the last half of the 16th century. He became a Catholic priest in 1536 when Scotland was one of the poorest and most backward countries in Europe. Knox protested against Roman Catholicism and joined the Reformation movement in 1546. After the reformers assassinated a Scottish cardinal, Knox and others were captured by the French who had aligned themselves with the Roman Catholic Church. After the English government obtained the release of Knox in 1549, he began preaching in England until Mary Tudor became queen in 1553 and established Roman Catholicism as the state religion in England. Knox fled as a religious refugee to the European continent where he met John Calvin in Geneva. Calvin influenced the young Knox, who returned to Scotland after the death of Queen Mary. Her successor, Queen Elizabeth, helped Knox and his associates overthrow the Catholic government of Mary, Queen of Scots; and Protestantism became the state religion of Scotland. From 1560 until his death in 1572, Knox was the most powerful political and religious leader in Scotland.[1]

A MAN OF GOD IS BORN

Nine generations later, on July 4, 1915, Emma Louise Lockett was born in Oklahoma City, Oklahoma, to Earl

McGrady Lockett and Almeda Estella White Lockett. Both grew up in northwestern Oklahoma on wheat farms. Earl Lockett became a Methodist preacher shortly after he and Almeda were married on July 11, 1907, and pastored several small Methodist churches in Oregon, Kansas, and Oklahoma. In 1914, they returned to Oklahoma City, where Earl became a fireman.

Emma graduated from Central High School in Oklahoma City in 1933 and took a job as an office girl and nurses' aide for a doctor. On a blind date in 1934, she met the tall, handsome, curly-headed Woodrow Wilson Stamps. "Woody," as he was known, was born July 23, 1913, in Wapanucka, Oklahoma, to Tilden Stamps and Lou Elliott Allen Stamps. Both were born in Texas but came to southern Oklahoma to farm shortly after their marriage in Wolfe City, Texas, on August 26, 1899.

Woody worked at the Dale Grocery Store in northwest Oklahoma City when he and Emma had the blind date at Northeast Lake. Within a few months, a serious relationship developed, and the question of marriage came up. Woody earned $12 a week and Emma brought home $10 a week. It became economically feasible for them to get married when some friends offered to let them move in with them and their parents. Woody and Emma were married at St. Luke's Methodist Church in Oklahoma City on May 8, 1936.

The housing arrangement with their friends lasted only three months. Woody began a new job as a milkman for Steffans Dairy so he and Emma could afford a garage apartment. Woody started his day long before dawn and delivered milk by horse and wagon. He didn't mind the long hours because he was making as much as $100 a month and could now comfortably support his wife and soon to be growing family.[2]

Donald Carrel Stamps was born at St. Anthony Hospital in Oklahoma City on November 10, 1938. His father Woody completed his route for the dairy and made it to the hospital in time to be with Emma when the baby came at 6:40 p.m.

A PROBLEM CHILD

By the age of two, it was apparent that Don was extremely independent and was going to be a problem child. He often wandered away from home on his tricycle when his mother allowed him outside the apartment to play. Emma usually found him playing in the park across the street. After several unsuccessful attempts to keep him in his own yard, Emma was forced to tie him to a long rope which was fastened to the clothesline. Don was perfectly happy to spend his outdoor play time in his sandbox within a few feet of the clothesline.

When he was four, the family moved to California to work in the shipyards. World War II was in full swing, and word had filtered back to Oklahoma that high paying jobs were in abundance in California. Woody and Emma had their second son, David Wayne Stamps on March 15, 1943, in Long Beach. Don started kindergarten in Wilmington and had problems from the very beginning.

His parents noticed he had difficulty speaking clearly. The impediment worsened, and Don began stuttering. He was embarrassed, and the stuttering made him insecure. The other children made fun of him, so Don fought back the only way he knew; he began stealing lunch money from his schoolmates. When the teacher caught him, he was kicked out of school. Once, he took his dad's new glasses outside and jumped up and down on them on the sidewalk until they were crushed into a thousand pieces. His parents couldn't figure out what was wrong.

Don's temper was explosive. Once, he was hitchhiking home from school. When a car failed to stop for him, he picked up a large rock and hurled it through the car's window. He was arrested and had to pay for the window. One day, Woody was using black paint on the window screens of the Stamps' house. When Woody went into the house for dinner, Don swiped the bucket and, for thirty minutes, painted a neighbor's white house. The once funny pranks and stunts had become a severe discipline problem.

Years later, after he became a missionary, Don looked back on his early years and said, "I believe from the very day I was born Satan had decided to ruin my life, to destroy my soul, to take me to hell, and to see me lost forever."[3]

By 1945, the war had ended and the lucrative wartime jobs in California dried up. The Stamps family moved back to Oklahoma City, where Woody joined forces with his brother James to start an upholstery business.

Don's stuttering didn't get any better. In the fourth grade the stuttering became worse, and Emma took him to a psychiatrist to discover the underlying cause of the stuttering. But the visits to the psychiatrist didn't help. Emma heard about a professor at the University of Oklahoma medical school who had done extensive study on stuttering. After a few visits to the professor, Don experienced some improvement and gained self confidence. However, the stuttering persisted and embarrassed him so much that he became an obstinate rebel by age twelve. He was so stubborn that he would not listen to his parents on any subject. The problem with Don was more serious than just a normal teenager with a streak of rebellion.

Emma occasionally attended the Linwood Methodist Church and thought church might help Don. One Sunday morning she dropped him off at Sunday school and gave him a dime for the offering. Don waved at his mom, went in the front door of the church, and then promptly left by way of the back door. The dime he had been given for the offering bought a cherry phosphate and a comic book at a nearby drugstore. After an hour, Don walked back to the church and was waiting at the front door when his mother picked him up. That "church experience" continued for several months. When they moved to Bethany, the family attended another local Methodist church for several years.

A third son, Robert Waybright Stamps, was born to Woody and Emma in Oklahoma City on January 15, 1950; and the family moved to N.W. 32nd and MacArthur. Emma had her hands full with a newborn baby, seven-year-old David, and a twelve-year-old boy who tested her patience daily. One of Don's good qualities at age twelve was his willingness to work. He mowed lawns in the neighborhood and picked up a job delivering the Oklahoma City Advertiser on Fridays. Weather never bothered him. When Friday came and his boss delivered the papers, Don threw the large bags on his lanky frame and made his rounds in sunshine, snow, or rain.

THE GANG DAYS

In junior high school, Don became a fighter. He would tear into friend or foe at the drop of a hat. He fought in the classroom, in the hallway, on the playground, or on the way home. His fighting reputation was widespread in the Putnam City school system. Younger brother David recalls the time when he was being picked on by another student on the schoolbus. A third student piped up, "You better leave him alone. That's Stamps' brother."[4]

Don began running around with a gang that made it a daily goal to plan some kind of mischief. He and six or seven other boys broke into a warehouse one night and stole hundreds of pounds of fireworks. The sky was lit up over northwest Oklahoma City for several nights until the stolen merchandise was used up. The gang used the fireworks to attack the homes of people they didn't like. They even threw bricks through plate glass windows of businesses and homes in the area.

Woody and Emma were trying their best at discipline. They tried talking, grounding, and sending Don to his room. When those forms of punishment didn't work, they resorted to using the belt on him. Don frustrated his dad so badly that Woody was often driven into a rage. Even during a severe whipping Don taunted his father with shouts of "Can't you hit any harder than that?" Don thought no one loved him even though his parents were doing everything they could to help him.

As Don advanced in his early teen years, the gang vandalism became worse. He and his friends would wreck anything for the fun of it. Once, after four nights of damaging several houses and businesses in the neighborhood, Don was faced with the glaring lights of five police cars. He was arrested and taken to jail. Later, Woody picked him up and took him home to his mother who met them at the door in tears.

Emma hated to answer the telephone during Don's junior high years. Many times, school officials called to ask her to pick him up immediately because he had been kicked out of class. He didn't like to study and was never prepared in class. His insecurity added to his problems and caused him to pull even more outrageous stunts. He turned the lawn sprinklers on during the annual Maypole dance. On one occasion, he slipped backstage in the school auditorium before a piano concert and placed several boxes of candles inside the piano. When the guest pianist tried to perform, only an occasional "plunking" sound came from the piano. Don once locked a horse in that same auditorium over the weekend. The place was a smelly disaster when the janitor opened the building on Monday morning.

Don's love for adventure came from reading about book characters like Mark Twain's Tom Sawyer and Booth Tarkington's Penrod. Even in his adult life, Don often said, "I'm always going to keep some of the little boy in me." He was right; but the road to maturity would be long and difficult for him.

During the summer before his fifteenth birthday, Don and a friend lied about their ages and joined the Air National Guard. They went to basic training, and the problems began. The drill instructor constantly cursed them. Don and his friend were ordered one afternoon to wash more than a thousand glass milk bottles and stack them by the mess hall door. They misunderstood the order and thought they were to wash and "break" the bottles by the door. The drill instructor was livid when he found a stack of broken bottles. He suspected the boys might be too young and called them into his office. When he discovered they were only fifteen, he took them under his wing until the end of basic training and sent them home.

By the time Don graduated from junior high school, all of his teachers had predicted he would end up in prison. He was caught stealing gas and spent much of his time in the principal's office. Don bragged that he held the Putnam City record for receiving 170 licks in a single school year. Woody and Emma had no idea what to do with him. Woody thought the conflict was so intense that surely Don would leave home and never come to see his parents again.

Don felt lost and unwanted. He felt he had no chance to succeed at anything.

Don Stamps needed a Savior.

PUSH BACK THE
DARKNESS

∽ *Chapter 3* ∾

The
Formative
Years

*I*t is not necessary or even ideal that a future man or woman of God go through a rebellious stage of life. Yet, God often takes the most unlikely candidates to demonstrate His amazing grace. The whole point of the gospel is that through the blood of Jesus Christ the most guilty of sinners can be converted into the most devoted saints.

GOD BEGAN TO TAKE CHARGE

At fifteen, Don's future looked dim. In the summer of 1954, he and his gang of friends continued to ravage northwest Oklahoma City. But God had a redemptive purpose for Don's life. When he seemed destined for serious trouble or tragedy, God sent a messenger in the form of the sixty- three-year-old Baptist grandfather of three of Don's closest friends.

Evan Jones had retired from his job as a truck driver for a local supply store. He was thin and short, a true Welshman. He had been faithful to God as a longtime member of the Capitol Hill Free Will Baptist Church in south Oklahoma City. The toes of his shoes were always turned up because he spent so much time on his knees in prayer. He was affectionately known as "Brother Jones." Three of his grandsons ran around with Don. The oldest, Richard Teas, was actually the leader of the gang that seemed headed for destruction. God used that connection to get Don in a position where the Holy Spirit could deal with him about his salvation.[1]

The Free Will Baptists trace their roots to the influence of Arminian-minded Baptists who migrated from England to the colonies. They taught free grace, free salvation, and free will. In the eighteenth century the denomination was organized into northern and southern branches. The Civil War and the issue of slavery prevented the groups from uniting until 1935 when the National Association of Free Will Baptists was organized at Nashville, Tennessee. The Free Will Baptists had grown to almost 250,000 members by 1980.[2]

Brother Jones and his wife were asked to stay with their grandsons while the boys' parents went on a short trip to Mexico just before school started. The Free Will Baptist Church began a revival about the same time, and Brother Jones felt God leading him to try to get his grandsons and their friends to the revival. Richard Teas and his brothers, Dean and Dan Tate, told Brother Jones how mean Don was and that Don would never go to church, much less be converted. Brother Jones was known for shutting himself in his closet to pray for three or four hours. He called himself "a fanatic for God" and decided he would fast and pray until the gang of boys went to church with him.

Brother Jones took his grandsons to church for the first four or five nights of the revival. All three went to the altar, repented, and accepted Jesus Christ as their personal savior. Don had not seen the boys for several days and went to their house to ask them to go to a John Wayne movie with him. The Tate boys and Richard Teas said, "Sure, we'll go to a movie. But first we have to go to church with Grandpa." Don hadn't been to church in years but didn't see how one service could be that bad. The boys piled into the back seat of the car and headed for the revival service.

DON STAMPS MEETS JESUS

Don sat between Brother Jones and Lowell Reed as the service began. Don wasn't listening to the songs or the preaching of the evangelist. He sat there saying over and over in his mind, "What a bunch of dummies!" Brother Jones noticed that Don wasn't listening and went to the back of the church where a faithful saint, Hally Lewis, sat. Brother Jones told her that Don desperately needed the Lord and asked her to begin praying immediately for him. Brother Jones returned to his seat and begged God for mercy for Don.[3]

Thoughts of the upcoming cowboy movie and popcorn and a Coke ran through Don's mind as the evangelist neared the end of the sermon. Don later recounted the miraculous events of the next hour:

"As soon as he quit preaching, I can't explain just what happened. All of a sudden, I guess the prayers of that old man and lady had gotten to God. The Holy Spirit came and convicted me. I knew nothing about the gospel or God or Jesus. I just knew that I was a sinner and was going to hell. The Holy Spirit was faithful. I stood there with my bottom lip trembling. Something went through my mind, saying, 'I've got to get saved! I've got to get saved! I've got to get saved!'

"I pushed old Brother Jones aside and burst out crying and bawling like I had never cried before. I was tough, but I was crying and headed for the altar. My soul cried out, 'Oh God, please forgive me!' He did! I was saved before I ever made the altar. A tidal wave of joy and peace and the presence of the Holy Spirit flooded across my soul. I fell across the altar and sobbed and wept and cried for joy. I kept saying, 'Somebody loves me, Somebody loves me, Somebody is going to help me. Somebody is going to redeem me and save me from myself, from the hate, the bitterness, and the sin. Somebody is going to rescue me from this life of death I am living!'

"Brother, there was not a thing in my life that was good. I wasn't worth a nickel. Everything was bad, but God reached down from heaven and took one poor, stupid, lost boy and saved me that night. I knew God in an instant. I had never met him before that night. It was just as if I had known him forever. He was my Father, and I was His son. I knew Jesus had died for me."[4]

Don wept at the altar for forty-five minutes. Pastor Ed Morris and the evangelist prayed with him. Lloyd Plunkett was two years older than Don and was sitting in the choir that momentous August night. Lloyd had last seen Don just before school was out in May. He was in agriculture class at Putnam City High School and heard an awful commotion outside. He looked out the window and saw Don yelling at the top of his voice at a vice principal who had just expelled him from school. Lloyd saw a different Don Stamps at the altar. Tears streamed down Don's face, and Lloyd knew something tremendous had happened.

When Don got up from the altar, everyone shook his hand. He was embarrassed. After the church service, Lloyd saw Don sitting on a car fender, away from the crowd and gazing "far away." Don got in the back seat of the car and wept all the way home.[5]

Woody and Emma were reading in the living room when Don walked in with red, swollen eyes. He told them, "I just got saved." He sat down in a rocking chair and related the story of his conversion. Woody and Emma were very happy and moved by Don's sincerity. That night and many nights thereafter they heard Don crying and praying late into the night.

That Baptist revival in the summer of 1954 had a lasting impact on Don and his friends. Seven boys—Richard Teas, Dean Tate, Dan Tate, Gene Mann, Lowell Reed, Wendell Payton, and Don—were converted because Brother Jones followed the leading of the Holy Spirit.[6]

Within a few days, Don showed up at Lloyd Plunkett's house with a thousand questions about God and the Bible. Don had always been inquisitive about any subject and now his complete attention was directed toward God. He and Lloyd would talk about the Bible late into the night. He wanted to know specific details about Christian beliefs. God had prepared young Lloyd with many of the answers, for he had given his life to Christ several years before and was a devoted student of the Bible. Lloyd would later graduate from a Freewill Baptist college in Nashville, Tennessee, and pastor churches in California and Washington.[7]

Don also spent a lot of quality time with Lloyd Plunkett's younger brother, Don. The two Dons were great outdoorsmen and loved to hunt deer, rabbits, and quail. One night while hunting rabbits in western Oklahoma City near Lake Overholser, a carload of boys looking for trouble began chasing Don Plunkett's 1957 Oldsmobile. The chase reached speeds of 110 miles per hour. Finally, the other car sped around Plunkett's car and blocked the roadway. Three burly guys got out of the car and lined up across the road. Don Stamps was upset and quickly got out of the car and pointed his shotgun at the three guys. They challenged Don, "What are you going to do, shoot us?" Don pulled out his pistol and shot three times directly in front of the three. Their eyes were as big as saucers as they scrambled for their car and sped off.

There was no doubt that Don's conversion had changed his life. Before his conversion, he had stolen an antique musket that was displayed over a neighbor's garage. After his conversion, Don cleaned and shined the rifle and delivered it in the dark of night to his neighbor's front porch.[8]

A BURDEN FOR SINNERS

Don cherished his visits with Brother Jones and Pastor Morris during his first few months as a Christian. He had an insatiable appetite for God's Word. His relationship with his parents improved drastically. There was no more stealing with the gang, as the gang now showed up regularly for church. Don lived for Sunday morning, Sunday night, and Wednesday night services. He prayed constantly for God to save other people.

Don felt such a burden for sinners that he talked to everyone he met about Jesus. During his first year as a Christian, he led more than a dozen of his friends to Christ. He still didn't know all the Christian terminology, so while praying for the Holy Spirit to convict the friends he brought to church he would simply pray, "Hit him God! Hit him God!" Don's boldness made him a great witness. Even with his stuttering, he would walk up to another student at school and say, "Hey, wouldn't you like to get saved?" If the friend said, "Maybe," Don replied. "Okay, I'll be by and pick you up, and we'll go to church."

Don really liked a particular painting of the Apostle Paul. He thought the painting captured the agony and burden that the apostle must have felt when he was writing to the churches. He had billfold-sized prints of the painting made at a local photography studio and gave them to his friends.

His scholastic achievements in high school were nothing to brag about, but he excelled in sports. He tried football for a short time, but found his place in track and field and for three years burned up the cinder tracks. He and Lowell Reed worked out every day for two or three hours. His training paid off. In his senior year, he finished second in the state in the mile run. He compared track with life itself, for he felt that the pain and effort necessary to finish the races he entered taught him perseverance and toughness.

THE YOUNG BUSINESSMAN

Don delivered newspapers for the *Daily Oklahoman* and the *Oklahoma City Times* from the age of eleven. He would pull younger brother David out of bed long before daylight on days he needed help with his route, and on Sundays they would begin folding papers at 5 a.m. Don used all forms of transportation to deliver both the morning and evening papers. In his earlier days he walked and threw a short route. As his need for more spending money grew, he bought a motor scooter and was given a longer route. For several years before he reached driving age he threw papers from a Harley-Davidson motorcycle. Then, with money saved from his paper routes, he bought an old Chrysler and took on two major routes from Bethany to Warr Acres, both suburbs of Oklahoma City. The car made it much easier on David to sit in the back seat and fold papers for Don to throw. Don's accuracy was phenomenal. After years of practice he could throw a paper from a speeding car to land exactly on target on his customer's front porch.[9]

One of Don's most unusual ways of getting the morning newspaper to his customers was by horse, for he always had been a cowboy at heart. He loved John Wayne movies and loved to shoot guns and pretend to be a fast-draw artist. When he was fifteen, he bought a horse named Cindy from a rancher near Norman. Don rode his motorcycle to Norman, broke Cindy in a half day, and rode her home. He pastured her in the Stamps' backyard, which had housed many of Don's wildlife projects down through the years. There had been rabbits, calves, pheasants, and mink. There was even a lamb that Don carried in the front door one night.

David was a valuable assistant in Don's newspaper organization. Because of his stuttering, Don was often afraid to approach a customer to collect the weekly paper bill. David was dispatched from the car to make the collection attempt.

Before Don's conversion, David was emotionally torn up much of the time because of the violent arguments between Don and his parents. As the second child, David took on the role of negotiator. However, when the fights began, David usually left the house. Don and his dad would soon forget what the previous fight had involved, but David sometimes took days to get over the scars of the latest family uproar.

David was totally opposite of Don. He would be saved at a Billy Graham crusade in Oklahoma City in 1956. He graduated from a Methodist seminary, St. Paul's School of Theology, in Kansas City, Missouri, and pastored two Methodist churches before changing careers to job counseling and his present occupation as a video producer. David and Don rarely agreed on theological issues. In fact, David became a Unitarian.

David's home life became more bearable as younger brother Bobby grew older. Now, Don picked on Bobby and left David alone. Being the youngest brother of Don Stamps was exciting for Bobby, who became Don's chief assistant in his many adventuresome projects.[10]

Don was unique in his approach to almost any problem. He bought several baby calves from a dairy one summer and placed them on a friend's ranch east of Norman. When the grass turned brown in the winter, the rancher called Don and told him to come get his calves. Don didn't have a pickup so he took the seats out of his four-door Ford and hauled the calves back to Bethany.

DEALING WITH HIS ANGER

Don and Lowell Reed were inseparable during their high school years. They were terrible students. Don's stuttering and Lowell's dyslexia interfered with their academic pursuits. Yet, they never missed school because they enjoyed each day in class. They found a grade school teacher during the summer to help them with their studies. Lowell Reed says he and Don "never really planned daily pranks but just took advantage of every opportunity that came along." Their pranks got them into so much trouble that when one of them did something wrong, the principal automatically sent for the other and punished them both.

Don loved to laugh. His pranks and his love for jokes kept everyone around him laughing. But Don's personality had a vicious side. Even after his conversion, Don was "a bundle of hostility." Problems from his childhood and rebellious teen years resulted in outbursts of anger even in later years. He developed a "philosophy of anger" and pledged to his friends that he would turn a negative into a positive by harnessing his anger to the cause of Christ. He would use his anger, then directed toward the enemies of Christ, to motivate him to persevere for his Lord in the face of severe adversity when other people would succumb to overwhelmingly discouraging circumstances.

One of Don's distinguishing characteristics after his conversion was his integrity. His extreme sincerity was reflected in his self-image and in the manner in which he presented himself to others. He would readily admit that some of his outbursts of anger were inappropriate and ill-timed, and that this flaw in his personality was something he needed to watch carefully throughout his life. He never excused or rationalized his shortcomings as a Christian.

On the other hand, he developed a strong conviction that there are specific occasions when Christians should express anger. His keen insight was that anger is an inevitable result of genuine Christian compassion. He identified numerous biblical examples in support of this contention. One of his favorites was the passage in Mark where the leaders in the synagogue were opposed to Jesus' healing the man with the withered hand because it was the Sabbath. Mark 3:5 says of Jesus that "after looking around at them with anger, grieved at their hardness of hearts, He said to the man, 'Stretch out your hand.' And he stretched it out, and his hand was restored."

Don believed Christians should get angry at evil as Jesus was and with false teachers as Paul was. Don's anger was now directed at wrongdoing and cruelty in the world. He was growing daily in his Christian walk.[11]

THE NAZARENE INFLUENCE

Don's formative years as a Christian were greatly influenced by his association with two strong Nazarene families. Identical twins, David and John Fine, who also had newspaper routes, first met Don when he rode his spotted pony into the newspaper distribution station.

Willard and Wilma Fine, parents of the twins, were strict members of the Church of the Nazarene who kept a close watch on their boys and prohibited them from playing cards, going to movies, and participating in other worldly activities. Even the twins' names, David Livingstone Fine and John Wesley Fine, were connected to great religious leaders. Don made himself at home with the Fines and spent much of his teenage years at the Fine house. The twins' sisters, Martha and Mary, always had plenty of lemonade and sandwiches for the boys. In fact, Don spent more time in his high school years at the Fines' than he did at his own house. He was always a night owl and would stay until the early morning hours when Mrs. Fine would stand by the door with his coat and hint strongly that he should go home. More than once the boys had to replace glass lightshades broken during wrestling matches in the living room. They even caved in the door of the refrigerator one night and had to use their paper route savings to buy Mrs. Fine a new door.[12]

The other Nazarene influence on Don came from his friend David Brown, known to his closest buddies as "Brownie." Don, the Fine boys, and Brownie became close friends. Don and David Fine weren't afraid to try anything once. John Fine and Brownie were practical thinkers who added a touch of reality to any stunt David and Don suggested.

The four friends loved to go to Turner Falls, a great swimming and recreation park about 60 miles south of Oklahoma City. The Fines and Don would decide on the spur of the moment to go to Turner Falls. They often went by Brownie's house, forced him into the back seat, and raced to Turner Falls with any car on the highway that would accept their challenge. Don's old Chrysler took almost more oil than gasoline to make the trip. Brownie was often the designated driver for the return trip while the other three boys slept in the back seat. One night, Brownie was so sleepy he couldn't drive anymore, so he pulled off the road and went to sleep. The boys awoke at daylight when cars began honking at them.[13]

Mrs. Fine spent many hours on her knees praying for the boys' safety because she knew how adventuresome and fearless they were.

Each day, the Fine twins and Don were up before daybreak to work their paper routes. They would return to the Fine house where Mrs. Fine always prepared breakfast. It took a pound of bacon, a loaf of bread, and a dozen eggs to satisfy the growing boys every morning.

Brownie and Don spent many hours talking about their future. Both were convinced they should be in some kind of Christian service, but neither knew exactly what he was supposed to do for God. Don was especially unsure because he continued to battle the stuttering problem. During high school, he worked very hard with speech therapists at the University of Oklahoma.

BECOMING A BIBLE CHRISTIAN

Don was now saved, but his love for practical jokes was still alive and well. Brownie, the Fines, and Don often swam in the buff at a deserted swimming hole on the North Canadian River. One afternoon David and Don slipped out of the river and stole John's clothing. John had to chase them across a field to get his clothing back.

"Court-busting" was a popular pastime of Don and the Fines. They would put red tape over the spotlight on Don's car and aggravate couples parked along the dark shores of Lake Overholser. Don would shine the spotlight on a car so the teenagers would get scared and leave the area. The stunt almost backfired one night when a teen jumped out of the car with a shotgun.

Don and David worked the entire summer of 1956 on a farm south of Norman, breaking horses and feeding the animals. David always thought Don had been born a hundred years too late because he loved the cowboy life so intensely.

Don was learning about Christian family life from being around the Fines and the Browns. Yet, he was far from the understanding and commitment to Christ that would qualify him for the spiritual tasks ahead. He saw that the two families lived daily the principles they talked about at church. Don was also good for the boys. His genuine zest for life gave David Fine a great deal of confidence. The four boys were constantly living life to the fullest and seeking adventure.

Don had an uncanny ability to shame his friends into performing dangerous stunts, but he didn't expect anyone to do anything that he wouldn't do first. It was not uncommon for Don to convince the Fine boys and Brownie to do such things as row across the lake at night or cross the river hanging from a cable. The friendship among the Fines, Don, and Brownie was solid and lasted through the years.

Today, David and John Fine are successful businessmen. David "Brownie" Brown graduated from Bethany Nazarene College and the University of Oklahoma, received his doctorate in plant physiology, and is now a professor at Point Loma College, a Nazarene school in San Diego, California.

Don was looking for guidance in his Christian life and saw the love and peace present in the Fine and Brown homes. In spite of the irony of his mischievous and adventuresome nature, he began to develop a high view of holiness. He wanted to know more about the Nazarene beliefs and doctrine and turned to books for the answer. There he was introduced to the writings of John Wesley and for a while spent every waking moment reading or talking on the subject. He adopted Wesley's statement about Christian fervor as his own creed:

"I am determined to be a Bible Christian; not almost, but altogether. Who will meet me on this ground? Join me on this or not at all."[14]

PUSH BACK THE DARKNESS

✐ Chapter 4 ✐

A Hunger for Holiness

When Don graduated from high school, he had no idea what direction God was going to lead him. Using his reputation as a track star, he entered Oklahoma State University in Stillwater, Oklahoma, in the fall of 1957. He moved all of his belongings to Stillwater in a new car that he had purchased with savings from a concrete finishing job and his paper routes.

Don was bored with his classes, and things didn't work out for him to become a member of the OSU track team. He completed the semester in Stillwater and went back to his parents' home in Oklahoma City. He decided to lay out of school for the spring semester and work long hours as a cement finisher. During that time, he was either working, praying, or reading dozens of books on the Bible, theology, or Christian biographies.

A MISSIONARY CALLING

One night in the spring of 1958, God spoke to Don as he prayed outside on the porch. Don began weeping and clearly heard God talk to him about preaching and being a missionary. He told God, "There's no way I can preach. I stutter so bad no one would listen to me. Man, I can hardly talk. Oh God, I can't do that!"[1]

Late one night Don was reading the biography of missionary David Livingstone, whom God had used in the nineteenth century to focus the world's attention on the needs of the African continent. Don identified with Livingstone, who was extremely temperamental and had so many personality flaws that hindered his ministry. Livingstone had beaten the odds to bring the gospel and modern medicine to the black continent. He became a national hero in England and, for a century, was called the greatest missionary in history. Livingstone was found dead kneeling beside his cot in Africa in 1873. The Africans so revered him that his heart was removed from his body and buried there. The rest of his body was mummified by the hot African sun and was sent back to England for a state funeral at Westminster Abbey in London.[2] Don bawled like a baby while he read the Livingstone story. By the time he finished the biography, he knew God was calling him specifically to be a missionary. He still stuttered and still questioned God about his abilities; but he remembered his glorious salvation experience and knew the least he could do was to dedicate his life to God's call.

There were questions that remained unanswered for Don. "How can I possibly get through school? How can I learn a foreign language?" He thought he had so little to offer God.

HIS NAZARENE BACKGROUND

Don had been introduced to the Nazarenes while running around with John and David Fine and David Brown. He decided to resume his college studies in the fall of 1960 at Bethany Nazarene College, located in the Oklahoma City suburb of Bethany, just a few miles from the Stamps home.

BNC had its beginnings as Oklahoma Holiness College in 1910 when early Nazarene leader C.B. Jernigan bought 160 acres and established the town of Bethany. In 1920, the school became known as Bethany-Peniel College and was designated as the official senior college for Nazarenes in the

South. In 1955, Nazarene leaders renamed the school Bethany Nazarene College. It is now known as Southern Nazarene University and is recognized as one of the finest religious educational institutions in the South.[3]

The Church of the Nazarene is a denomination that grew from the preaching of the doctrine of entire sanctification as taught by John Wesley in the eighteenth-century revival in England. The restoration of sinful men to holiness of heart and life was the central message taught by Wesley. He vigorously defended his position that Jesus dying on the cross was the only source of grace from God that could save a fallen man. Wesley taught that even when a man was saved he continued to daily fight his mortal flesh and needed a second distinct experience of grace called entire sanctification, which decisively dealt with man's sinful nature and purified the heart.

Just before the Civil War split America apart, a great revival swept the country. Beginning in 1858, hundreds of daily prayer meetings across the northeastern part of the United States inspired Christians to seek holiness of heart and life. There was a moral and spiritual crisis in the country after the bloody Civil War, and Methodist preachers in the North and the South called for a return to their Wesleyan tradition of holiness. The holiness revival continued for almost thirty years. Out of Methodism came at least a dozen Wesleyan denominations, of which the Nazarenes were the largest and most prominent.

Dr. Phineas F. Bresee was a renowned Methodist preacher for the last forty years of the nineteenth century. He taught with fervor the Wesleyan doctrine of entire sanctification. He and his Methodist superiors drifted apart over many issues in the 1890's; and by 1900 Bresee was considered a central figure in the American holiness revival. Under his leadership, the Church of the Nazarene was organized nationally at a meeting at Pilot Point, Texas, in 1908. The new denomination was made up of several associations of churches that had resulted from the spiritual awakening of the holiness revival.[4]

Don liked what he heard about the Nazarenes and their holiness lifestyle. He plunged into his studies at Bethany Nazarene College with a passion for learning the truth about the Bible and its teachings. At first he wanted to follow in the footsteps of his missionary hero David Livingstone as a medical missionary. His plans to be a missionary suffered a setback when his counselor at BNC discouraged him from attempting any kind of public ministry. The counselor thought Don's stuttering was so severe that he could never be a successful communicator. Despite the counselor's advice, every time Don thought about quitting he was reminded of God's definite call on his life. He was unbending in his perseverance and promised God that he would do everything possible to carry the message of the gospel to other lands.

LIFELONG FRIENDS

Don was blessed with great Christian friends at BNC. Through David and John Fine, he met their cousin Larry, who transferred to BNC from Southwest Missouri State University. Years later, after Larry completed his education, he became a professor of pastoral counseling, spiritual formation, and Christian doctrine at Mid-America Nazarene College in Olathe, Kansas, where he has taught for almost a quarter century. At BNC, Don, Larry Fine, and Larry's roommate Dick Bond became close friends. Larry, a fifth generation Nazarene, calls his college friendship with Don one of the best things that ever happened to him:

"Don was very strict in his studies, was a nut about Greek, disciplined to the hilt. When 10 p.m. came, though, he was through studying. I always knew who was running up the dorm steps. Don came by the dorm almost every night. He was already very missions-minded and serious about his service for God. He was strict in his beliefs and never changed from the day I met him to the day he died. He was an avid reader, and I learned a lot about God because of Don's many questions. He thought of topics to study and debate that had never crossed my mind. Meeting Don and Dick, who later became the student body president at BNC, was crucial to my future as a Christian."[5]

Don also became friends with Charles Pickens, Bill Bowden, and Carl Godwin. Carl had been called to preach at age sixteen after being reared in a Nazarene home. Jim Dimick was his roommate at BNC. Carl recalls the great theological arguments between Don and Jim, heated discussions that lasted into the wee hours of the morning:

"I would sit back and watch Jim and Don go at it. They would talk about John Wesley and sinless perfection. Don hated liberalism. If some professor had made a liberal comment during that day's class, Don was on the warpath. The debates would go on for hours. They would get so mad at each other, but when the debate was over, they were friends. They used their Bibles, flipping them back and forth. Jim would tell Don he had the brains of a ball bearing. Don would often comment, 'Are you ignorant?'"[6]

Godwin, who is senior pastor of a large independent Baptist church that he founded in Lincoln, Nebraska, still uses Don's statement—"The Bible is the Bible is the Bible, the total authority."

The heavy theological debates that Jim and Don staged overflowed from the dorm room to Sam's Coffee Shop on N.W. 39th Street near the BNC campus. Don would look Godwin in the eye and demand that he account for his future...now. Don wanted to know everyone's calling and vision. He thought big. He was ready to change a whole nation for God. His positive vision made a great impact on those around him.

Dan Davis was a special friend to Don during their undergraduate days. Dan was born in India to missionary parents, Roy and Dewdrop Davis. Don took the opportunity to ask many questions of Dan and another "missionary kid," Stephen Heap. Dan served for many years as a medical missionary in Africa. He presently is a medical doctor specializing in pathology in Anchorage, Alaska. He recalls the nightly visits of Don to the dorm:

"Sam's was our little hang-out, a donut for a nickel and a cup of coffee for a nickel. Since refills were free, we stayed half the night. About bedtime, Don would show up outside our window yelling, 'Fools!' He got the phrase from the apostle Paul's saying he was a 'fool' for the sake of Christ. Don yelled that everywhere we went."[7]

Dan, Jim Dimick, and Don once decided to go on a fast. Don challenged them to fast if they "were really serious about finding a deeper walk with the Lord." Dan recalls, "I thought I was going to die. I had terrible headaches. But we toughed it out three or four days. Don wanted to go for a week or a month. We fasted that week in all the sincerity we could muster."

Two professors at BNC influenced Don greatly in the initial formation of his theology of holiness and living a separated life. Dr. W.N. King and Dr. Donald Metz spent hours, in class and out of class, discussing the Bible with him. Both professors believed strongly that Christians should be a separated people and that holiness in one's heart and life was absolutely necessary to live a victorious Christian life. Dr. Metz, the chairman of the Religion Department at the college, vividly remembered Don as a student:

"I remember his intensity. He usually sat near the front of the class and loved to jump into any discussion during the class time. His stuttering problem was noticeable but never seemed to inhibit him in debates. Don would challenge me a lot in class. He was not obnoxious but enthusiastically involved. Don and Larry Fine spent many Thursday and Friday afternoons in my office discussing or debating some biblical topic."[8]

Don became very emotional when anyone doubted the absolute inspiration and inerrancy of the Bible. When Dr. Metz tried to present the liberal view of the inspiration or non-inspiration of the Bible, Don would object strenuously, labeling such lectures as a "waste of time." Despite the objections, Dr. Metz calls Don one of his all-time favorite students in his thirty-five years of teaching religion at BNC and Mid-America Nazarene College. Dr. Metz's opposition to liberal trends within the Nazarene denomination won him high respect from Don and "the Bethany boys" who hung around with him.

Another positive influence on Don's life in college was his friendship with Lawrence Williams. Lawrence was blind and needed someone to read Greek aloud to him so he could complete his homework assignments. Don volunteered, and a lifelong friendship was born. Don had excelled in his Greek classes, and the professors often called on him to tutor other students. Don would show up nightly at Lawrence's dorm room, or later at Lawrence's apartment after he was married, to pace the floor and read Greek. Don was like a caged lion. He never stuttered while reading the complex Greek, but the stuttering was terrible when he turned to normal conversation.

Don was an intense student. Before a major exam he would spend three or four days doing nothing but studying. After the test he would tell Lawrence—half jokingly and half seriously—"Well, Williams, I can now get back to being spiritual again."

Don and Lawrence shared more than their Greek studies. They both believed in strong biblical standards of holiness, including the inerrancy of the Bible, modest dress, and separation from the spirit of the world. One semester a professor at BNC made a statement that some of the stories of the Bible, such as Jonah and the whale, are only myths. Don and Lawrence were outraged. They circulated a petition that dozens of students signed. The petition, supporting the full inspiration and inerrancy of the Bible and calling for the dismissal of the professor, was forwarded by Dr. Metz to BNC president Dr. Roy Cantrell and the Board of Trustees. The petition drive was a vivid example of how Don felt about the absolute truth and inspiration of the Bible.[9]

ALONG CAME LINDA

Up to this time, girls had never played an important role in Don's life. Perhaps his stuttering was a factor. He would rather spend time with his friends or debating the Bible with his professors. All that changed during "Twirp Week" at

BNC in the spring of 1964. During "Twirp Week" girls were allowed to ask boys for dates. Don was twenty-five years old and a senior. The girl who entered his life was Linda Kathleen Sodowsky, a cute and petite nineteen-year-old sophomore.

Linda was born in Nampa, Idaho, on September 14, 1944, to Nazarene Pastor Paul Milford Sodowsky and Kathleen Earl O'Hara Sodowsky. Paul was born in Blackwell, Oklahoma. His father was an unsaved oil field worker, but young Paul had a godly Nazarene grandfather who lived on a nearby farm and helped direct Paul to church and to Bethany-Peniel College where he met Kathleen. They were married in 1938. After successful pastorates in Texas, Kansas, and Missouri, Paul took a position in the Department of Benevolence at the world headquarters of the Church of the Nazarene in Kansas City, Missouri. Linda completed high school at Southeast High School in Kansas City in 1962 and arrived at Bethany Nazarene College with a call from God to the mission field already upon her life.

Linda was saved at age four during a revival in her father's church. She had a storybook childhood with absolutely no problems. When she was twelve, a missionary spoke at church, and that night God placed a missions call in her heart.

A few months before her first date with Don, Linda had a decision to make. It was time to choose a major at BNC. She had to decide what direction to take. A missionary preached on campus, and Linda felt she must definitely accept the call to the mission field or lose her salvation. She went back to her dorm room, laid across the bed, and promised God that she would go wherever He wanted her to go, even if she had to go alone.

Linda really didn't know much about Don when they had their first date. He was one of about 1,200 students at the college. He lived off campus with his parents, and she lived on campus in the girls' dorm. However, she knew from Larry Fine and other friends that Don wanted to be a missionary.[10]

Don was "set up" by several of his friends to be in Ron Phillips' room in the dorm at a certain time when Linda planned to call. The phone rang, and Linda nervously asked for Don. She introduced herself as a member of the Mission Band and asked him for a date. To everyone's surprise, Don accepted. A few minutes later, Don showed up at Lawrence and Martha Williams' apartment, loudly complaining about how he had been set up.[11]

The night of the date arrived; and Don and Linda double-dated with Ron Phillips and his date Mary Smith, who later became his wife. They attended a college function and ate Mexican food. After the evening with Don ended, Linda had no idea what would happen next. She couldn't sleep. What if Don never asked her out again?

Linda was studying organ that semester and practiced on the large pipe organ in the Fine Arts Building one or two hours every day. She often sat at the organ dreaming how wonderful it would be if Don Stamps would walk through the door and ask her out.

A week after the first date, Don came through the door of the auditorium. Linda's heart was pounding as he asked her for a date to the Heart Pal Banquet, but she already had a date. She was afraid Don wouldn't ask her again after she had to refuse him, but he did and they dated for two and a half years before they were married.

Don nicknamed Linda "Gumpers." They had a solid relationship and were very much attracted to each other.

However, Don's strong beliefs interfered with their relationship when Linda was a candidate for homecoming queen at BNC. Don thought queen competitions were carnal and contrary to Jesus' teachings about humility. He tried to talk Dan Davis and other friends into putting a skunk in a burlap bag and throwing it into the gym during the coronation ceremony. They refused and Don reluctantly showed up to escort Linda.

DON AND DIMICK

In May, 1964, Don graduated from BNC with a bachelor's degree in religion. He worked long, hard hours in the concrete finishing business again that summer to save enough money for school expenses so that he wouldn't have to work during the next school year. He stayed an extra year at BNC to earn a master's degree in religion. It was during that year that Don and Jim Dimick became close friends.

Dimick firmly believed that God had called him to be a theologian and college professor. He and Don were alike in many ways. They had been wild teenagers, had vicious tempers, were always ready to fight, were adventuresome, and loved nature. Both were night owls and independent. Neither followed the herd. They loved the Scriptures and looked forward to "locking horns" in a spirited theological debate. Because they were both genuine mavericks, Don and Dimick were inseparable.

As a new friend, Dimick became another potential victim of Don's pranks. Dimick had been reared in Maine and came to BNC knowing very little about Oklahoma and the "wild West." His only knowledge of Oklahoma came from his brother, who had read detective magazines and warned him to be careful because there were a lot of murders taking place

in the West. His fear of being shot and killed in a wild frontier and newspaper accounts of a vigilante committee being
organized to assist the police to catch muggers hiding in the
woods around Lake Overholser set him up for one of Don's
all-time great pranks, commonly called "The great gunfight
at the North Canadian River."

Don and Dimick were driving around the backroads near
the river and lake looking for a spot for a campfire. Don kept
talking about what a "spooky" night it was. He showed
Dimick where he kept his pistol under the dashboard of his
car. Dimick's fears had increased when they passed another
car on the lonely road, and Don made up a story about a
jilted boyfriend who had shot at several people in the area.

Unknown to Dimick, Bill Bowden was hiding in the
woods near the edge of the river. As Don and Bowden had
prearranged, Bowden fired a rifle with blanks and Don pre-
tended to be shot. Their plan was for Dimick to run back to
the car and retrieve Don's pistol that also had been loaded
with blanks. But, the carefully laid plan went haywire. Don
had underestimated just how afraid Dimick was of being shot.

As the shots from Bowden's rifle rang out, Dimick broke
into a dead run for cover. He knew he had to go for help
since he thought Don was wounded. There was no way he
would try to get Don's gun from the car because the shots
had come from the area where the car was parked. Dimick
ran down the dirt road until he saw the beacon from nearby
Wiley Post Airport. Fearing that the "nut with the gun"
might see him on the road, he took off through the woods
toward the airport beacon. He ran through a creek and stum-
bled face first into a barbed wire fence. He tore a gash in
his cheek and ripped his new coat into shreds. He finally
found what he thought was a paved road. It was actually the

runway of the airport. He ran down the middle of the runway to the control tower. It was empty.

He tried to flag down cars on a nearby street. Finally a police car stopped, and Dimick told the officers about his "wounded" friend. He accompanied the officers in searching the lake area for the supposedly wounded Don. One policeman knew Don's propensity for major pranks and suspected a hoax. The police finally saw Don's car and stopped him. After Don admitted the prank, Dimick was taken to the local hospital where it took twenty stitches to repair the cuts on his face.[12]

Don and Dimick spent many hours browsing through used bookstores in the Oklahoma City area. BNC professors directed Don to many classic religious books that molded his deep beliefs. Don especially loved books about missionaries and soul-winning. He read about the lives of Charles Spurgeon, Charles Finney, and D.L. Moody. He was impressed by the story in Billy Graham's biography of how Dr. Graham walked around a golf course near Wheaton College for hours, praying. Don learned from his reading that prayer was the key to successful soul-winning. He was particularly impressed with the writings of C.S. Lewis, Leonard Ravenhill, Oswald J. Smith, James Stewart, E. Stanley Jones, and Andrew Murray. One of Don's favorite books was *Shadow of the Almighty*, the life story of martyred Missionary Jim Elliot, written by his widow, Elisabeth Elliot.

Don identified with Jim Elliot. Both loved Christ and lost souls with a passion. They were both "fearless" and had an adventuresome outlook on life. Don underlined key passages of Elliot's philosophy in the book. One can look at Don's copy of the book today and discover how he believed so strongly in the power and necessity of prayer. On page after page Don wrote comments and "starred" sections on Elliot's call to the mission field. He double-underlined Elliot's statement that "if he stayed in the United States [as a minister] the burden of proof would lie with him to show that he was justified in doing so."[13]

The adventuresome and "cowboy" side of Don sometimes took a back seat to oil painting and classical music. Don had been gifted as an artist since childhood. He would look at a photograph and amazingly transfer the scene to his canvas. Once he started a painting, he didn't quit. It was not uncommon for him to paint all night.

Don used his love for classical music to make a point about the proper way to preach. He told Dimick that a sermon is like a Beethoven symphony. It begins with a slow, soft beat, gets louder and faster, and ends with a loud crescendo. Don believed a preacher should bring his sermon to a dramatic, climactic finish, to stir the people and move them to make a positive decision for Christ. Don would play the symphony ending to Dimick over and over again to make his point.

Don and Dimick loved the outdoors. On weekends during the warm months they would stay up all night discussing the latest books they had read. These "all-nighters" were usually conducted around a campfire on the bank of a river or lake. It was during those deep discussions that Dimick learned so much about Don:

"Don's indelible conviction was that every word of Scripture was inspired by God; therefore, the Bible was for him the absolute authority in his life. However, what really distinguished Don from most other Christians was an all-consuming passion to bring both his beliefs and practices into total conformity with God's written Word as the Holy

Spirit enabled him to understand it. He would have no compromise with what he perceived to be the clear teachings of the Scripture. I never met a person who was more devoted to living out the true meaning of the biblical faith."

"Don was brilliant and analyzed issues in great depth. He possessed the mind of a theologian. First and foremost, he saw himself as a man called by God to bring the gospel message to the ends of the earth. He carried a heavy burden for lost souls. Because he took the Bible with such dreadful seriousness, he accepted the reality of hell and wanted to do something in his power to help people avoid that horrible place."[14]

Don was haunted by the immense suffering he saw in the world. At times he had a problem reconciling the horror of suffering with his belief in a sovereign, loving God. Dimick remembers the all-night sessions around the campfire on that subject:

"We invested more time wrestling with this issue than with any other topic. Our only comfort was found in the person of Jesus Christ and the cross. The living God had not remained aloof, but had become incarnate in Jesus and had suffered and died for us in order to bring redemption and an end to the misery that resulted from sin and evil. I will always believe that God's mysterious providence was at work in those days preparing Don for the terrible ordeal that lay ahead for him. His faith withstood satanic attacks upon the goodness of God because of his confidence in the promises of his Lord."[15]

MORE AND MORE QUESTIONS

Don began questioning the official position of the Church of the Nazarene on several subjects while still in college at BNC. He wrote his master's thesis on church

growth in Brazil and began to drift toward a position agree-
ing with Pentecostals on the gifts of the Holy Spirit. He
read *New Patterns of Church Growth in Brazil* by William R.
Read. The book presented an in-depth analysis of missionary
efforts and concluded that the future of evangelism in Brazil
belonged to the Assemblies of God because of its emphasis
on the Holy Spirit. While Don was reading Read's book, he
began thinking about Brazil as a possible place for service
as a missionary. During his research on the thesis, conversations with Dimick turned to Pentecost:

"Don, the 'soul-winner,' was elated by the church growth
figures arising out of the Pentecostal Movement in Brazil.
His enthusiasm for the Pentecostal success was met with
disdain by his examination committee. Don was visibly
shaken when he explained to me that those three Nazarene
professors [on the committee] would not give the
Pentecostals any credit whatsoever. He just could not understand the Nazarene animosity toward those people. He did
not contemplate a move to Pentecostalism at that point in
time, but he had formulated a very favorable opinion of the
whole movement. No one could get away with 'Pentecostal
bashing' in Don's presence. He would come to their defense
at the drop of a hat. He had such a strong passion for effective evangelism that the seed had been planted in those
early years for his eventual participation in this great
Christian movement."[16]

Don and Linda became engaged at the end of the spring
semester in 1965. Linda then began her senior year at BNC,
while Don made plans to attend seminary at the Nazarene
Theological Seminary in Kansas City.

PUSH BACK THE
DARKNESS

❧ *Chapter 5* ❧

The
Seminary
Years

*D*on began seminary still unsure exactly where God was leading him. He knew for certain that he was called to be a missionary, but God had not told him where or when. He still had doubts about his stuttering and questioned how God could use him on a mission field.

JOHN WESLEY ADAMS

A friendship with fellow seminary student John Wesley Adams became one of the most important relationships in Don's life. He had actually met Wesley during their undergraduate days at BNC, but their real friendship developed in seminary. Wesley was born in Wheatland, Wyoming, on August 3, 1941. His father, J. Kenneth Adams, and mother, Ella, pastored Nazarene churches in Colorado, New Mexico, Texas, and Oklahoma.

Wesley was saved at an early age but drifted away from God during his teen years and became involved with the wrong crowd. After the junior-senior prom at El Reno, Oklahoma, on May 17, 1958, Wesley and several friends were drinking and driving to Roman Nose State Park near Watonga, Oklahoma, for a weekend party. Wesley was asleep in the back seat when the driver lost control of the car on a sharp curve. As the car skidded out of control and rolled over in the darkness of the Oklahoma night, Wesley was awakened by the sounds of screeching tires, twisting metal, and breaking glass. When the wrecked vehicle came to rest, all four of Wesley's friends crawled out of the mangled car amazingly with only minor injuries. Wesley did not have a scratch on the outside of his body, but his neck had been broken and his spinal cord injured. He was unable to move. He had been instantly paralyzed from the chest down.

For thirty-six hours the doctors at an Oklahoma City hospital didn't think Wesley would live. He was suffering from asthma, pneumonia, and complications from the paralysis. His mother stayed at his bedside during those critical hours and remained in constant intercessory prayer for the life of her rebellious teenage son. At one point, she saw demons come to the foot of Wesley's bed. They said, "We've come to take him away." She resisted the demons and continued to intercede with God on Wesley's behalf.

Two days after the accident, Wesley began improving physically, and his mother talked frankly with him about his salvation. Wesley broke down and wept and asked God for forgiveness and restoration. God's presence came and filled the hospital room. It was like someone had turned on a floodlight in the room, and Wesley joyfully and spontaneously began singing "Amazing Grace" and other hymns. The intercession of Ella Adams was the difference between life and death for Wesley.

Wesley, paralyzed and unable to move, was strapped to a stryker frame for six weeks. Afterwards, he was placed in a body cast and spent almost eighteen months in hospitals and rehabilitation. While in the Children's' Convalescent Hospital in Bethany, Oklahoma, Wesley had several visits from God. During the lonely nights lying in a dark ward, Wesley heard God speak clearly to him, reassuring him of His love and desire to guide Wesley's life.

Wesley graduated from Bethany High School in May, 1960. He then enrolled at Bethany Nazarene College, with plans to be a lawyer. However, in his first month as a history major at BNC, God began speaking to Wesley about yielding his life to become a full-time minister of the gospel. One night the presence of God was awesome in his room and the Lord dealt tenderly with Wesley about the ministry. He was afraid because of his handicap. The call seemed unreasonable, and Wesley struggled with it for about six weeks. He was embarrassed to tell anyone about the special call from God. When he did disclose it to his rehabilitation counselor, he received a negative response. The counselor had urged Wesley to select a well-paying occupation that could be performed from a wheelchair. That was the primary reason Wesley had decided to study law. The counselor cautioned him about pursuing the ministry, about the unusual expenses of being a quadriplegic and how difficult it would be for Wesley to earn a decent living as a preacher in a wheelchair. Whenever Wesley was tempted to be discouraged about his decision, the Lord would bring great peace and reassurance that the call to the ministry was the correct path for his life.[1]

KINDRED SPIRITS

Don and Wesley were kindred spirits. They both abhorred compromise and liberalism in Christianity and stood together strongly for righteousness and truth. Both were ready to go through war and battle for those two issues. Wesley had also been involved in the famous petition drive against liberal professors at BNC.

In seminary, Wesley still had a manual wheelchair, and Don was always available to physically assist Wesley and help him with buildings that did not have wheelchair ramps.

Linda was still in Bethany at BNC during Don's first seminary year; thus Don and Wesley had extra time to develop their friendship. They talked many hours about theology, the Bible, and their desire for a deeper relationship with God. Don wondered why God seemed so far away at times. He had experienced such a sovereign visitation of God the night he was saved and longed for a continuous closeness to God of that magnitude.

Both Don and Wesley desperately sought God for the release of healing for Wesley. They read books on divine healing, studied the Scriptures on the subject, and launched an all-out effort to give God the opportunity to heal. They watched the newspaper in Kansas City for healing revivals, and Don took Wesley to healing services. They heard about great miracles happening in Indonesia and talked about ways to raise money to send Wesley over there. They strongly believed God could heal Wesley and often prayed for the answer. The healing did not come, but they did not waver in faith toward God or about the teaching of Scripture on healing.

They attended Grandview Church of the Nazarene in Grandview, Missouri, a suburb of Kansas City. The pastor, Ray Lunn Hance, was a fellow BNC graduate. During Wesley's senior year at seminary, he conducted a week of revival services at the Grandview church. Much prayer preceded the special week of services. Wesley and others believed he would be healed during the revival. In the final Sunday night service, Pastor Hance, Don, and others in the church gathered around Wesley and prayed. Don held Wesley up physically for an extended period of time while the prayer meeting continued. Still, Wesley's healing did not come.[2]

During seminary, a brilliant science student named Rodger Young became close to Don. Don's inquisitive nature resulted in a thousand questions to Rodger about scientific subjects, for he wanted to know how everything worked.

Rodger was born in Michigan, earned an undergraduate degree at Reed College in Portland, Oregon, and was selected to receive the prestigious Rhodes Scholarship to study physical mathematics at Oxford University in England. He came from a non-Christian family and became an intellectual Buddhist at Oxford. One summer he was hitchhiking in Germany and met some missionaries who witnessed to him. A few weeks later he was saved in a Church of England revival back at Oxford. After serving two years in the U.S. Army, Rodger entered the Nazarene Seminary in Kansas City. Rodger described Don's innermost thoughts and questions during the first year of seminary:

"Don wanted to be consistent. He wanted consistency in God and consistency among people who followed God. Don had really gone through an extensive period of doubting God. He had been through his darkest days of this kind of questioning before seminary, but he still would ask me questions and wrestle with the whole idea of God's existence. One night he specifically resolved for himself the question of death. He said death must not be so bad because God is love. Even during seminary Don was a thorough, systematic theologian. He would not accept "pat" or easy answers. He didn't understand why church members were taught to dress modestly in principle but in practice the standard was thrown to the wind when it involved the public swimming pool. He greatly disliked such inconsistency."[3]

But Don didn't spend all his time at seminary in serious reflection. Frequently he turned to his old pranks. One night Don, Ron Wilson, and Rodger went to the Paseo section of Kansas City and climbed to the top of some tall trees. Don preached from the treetop in his loudest voice to everyone who passed by.

Don's first formal preaching experience during seminary was at the downtown Rescue Mission in Kansas City. Wesley was present for Don's first sermon:

"He preached for a long time that night. He really got wound up. One guy went to sleep and fell out of his chair. That didn't deter Don. He overcame his stuttering and somehow got the message through. Our hearts were thrilled when several men responded to the altar call."[4]

THE CALL TO BRAZIL

Don's favorite subject in seminary was missions. Dr. Paul Orjala was the gifted professor who had been given the task to train potential missionaries at the Nazarene Seminary. Orjala had been a successful Nazarene missionary in Haiti and was a walking encyclopedia of where revivals were breaking out around the globe. His class time was spent closely analyzing why God was moving in certain countries. Don, Wesley, and Rodger heard Dr. Orjala describe the great revival that was sweeping Indonesia in the mid-1960's. The three students got so excited about their desire to see God do something in a big way that they talked about going to Indonesia together and studying the language. But when Dr. Orjala began a series of lectures on the Pentecostal revival explosion in Brazil, Don knew that Brazil was the country where he would someday preach the gospel.

Immediately, Don began to carry a heavy burden for Brazil. He read everything about Brazil that he could get his hands on. He asked questions in class until Dr. Orjala had to ask him to make an appointment in his office to continue the quest for more information. Don thought often about Brazil during those seminary days.[5]

Brazil was a country dominated by the Roman Catholic Church when the first Pentecostal missionaries arrived in 1910. The story of how God sent Gunnar Vingren and Daniel Berg to Brazil is one of the most exciting and glorious stories in the history of missions. Vingren was a Swedish-born pastor of a small Pentecostal church in South Bend, Indiana. He had received the baptism in the Holy Spirit on a visit to his native Sweden. One Saturday night during a prayer meeting, Adolph Ulldin began to prophesy under the power of the Holy Spirit. He said to Vingren, "You are to go to Para to teach the people there about the Lord. Your food will be simple, but God will give you everything you need." Then Brother Ulldin spoke in Portuguese, the language of Brazil. Vingren nor anyone in the congregation knew where Para was located. Vingren thought Para was surely a town in rural Indiana or maybe in Illinois. He went to a library and discovered that Para is a state in northern Brazil. The next Saturday night at a prayer meeting Brother Ulldin again prophesied, this time to another Swede, Daniel Berg. He told Berg that he was to go with Vingren to Para. He even gave them the date they were to sail for Brazil from New York City.

In November, 1910, Vingren and Berg arrived in Belem, the capital city of Para. They had very little money, so Berg took a job in a foundry to pay for Portuguese lessons for Vingren. At night, Vingren taught Berg what he learned that day in language school. Their food and lodging was pitiful, but the two young missionaries knew they were in the will of God.[6]

They held prayer meetings in the basement of a Baptist church. Soon Brazilians began receiving the baptism in the Holy Spirit as the believers did on the Day of Pentecost.

The Baptists did not believe in speaking in tongues so the fledgling ministry of Vingren and Berg had to move out of the basement. In June, 1911, eighteen Brazilians became the first Assemblies of God members in Brazil. The Pentecostal revival had begun. The Swedish Assemblies of God sent several Swedish missionaries to help Vingren and Berg.

Mr. and Mrs. Frank Salter were the first American Pentecostal missionaries in Brazil when they arrived in 1934. They went to Brazil under the sponsorship of another church but received the baptism in the Holy Spirit shortly after their arrival. They were then appointed missionaries by the General Council of the Assemblies of God in Springfield, Missouri. Other Americans responded to the call to take the gospel to Brazil. Churches were established in all sections of the country, including the remote interior. A publishing house was established and radio ministries were begun. By 1965, there were millions of members of the Brazilian Assemblies of God.[7]

The Church of the Nazarene sent Earl and Gladys Mosteller as its first missionaries to Brazil in 1958. Their work experienced some success and a number of churches had been established with primarily Brazilian national pastors.

As Don and Wesley continued to search for more of God in seminary, they saw a dimension of spiritual reality and ministry, especially in the revival in Brazil, that was not being addressed in Nazarene Seminary. They read *The Cross and the Switchblade* by David Wilkerson and regretted that the Nazarenes did not generally believe in the supernatural manifestation of the Holy Spirit. They began earnestly seeking an answer.

PUSH BACK THE DARKNESS

~ *Chapter 6* ~

Filled with the Holy Spirit

*D*on's and Wesley's spiritual struggles were not over, but they had come a long way since they began seminary. Their quest for healing and insatiable thirst for true experiences with God had led them far from traditional Christianity. Knowing Wesley had brought a greater sense of responsibility into Don's life, and Wesley's friendship with Don had opened up the life of the wheelchair-confined young man to a broader world of ideas and activities.

A THIRST FOR GOD

God honored the hunger and thirst of Don and Wesley for more of the reality of the Holy Spirit and His power in their lives during their seminary studies. Their Nazarene background had taught them that the Holy Spirit convicted men of sin and lived in the hearts of believers after conversion. The Nazarenes and other holiness denominations usually interpreted "being filled with the Spirit" to mean the believer's "entire sanctification." Many other denominations have typically understood this as referring to the infilling of the Holy Spirit that accompanies true conversion. On the other hand, Pentecostal churches believe that the baptism in the Holy Spirit is a distinct, separate, empowering experience of the Holy Spirit available to all born-again believers after their conversion.

At the turn of the century when Pentecostal organizations began forming, Dr. R.A. Torrey, the first head of the

Moody Bible Institute, explained the difference between regeneration and the baptism in the Holy Spirit:

"It is evident that the baptism with the Holy Spirit is an operation of the Holy Spirit distinct from and additional to His regenerating work.... A man may be regenerated by the Holy Spirit and still not be baptized with the Holy Spirit. In regeneration, there is the impartation of life by the Spirit's power, and the one who receives it is saved; in the baptism with the Holy Spirit, there is the impartation of power, and the one who receives it is fitted for service."[1]

Dr. A.B. Simpson, the founder of the Christian and Missionary Alliance, used the life of Jesus to support his belief that the baptism was a distinct work of the Holy Spirit:

"First, He was born of the Spirit, then He was baptized by the Spirit, and then He went forth to work out His life and ministry in the power of the Spirit.... Born like Him of the Spirit, we, too, must be baptized by the Spirit, and then go forth to live His life and reproduce His work."[2]

The first time in history that God made the baptism in the Holy Spirit available to all believers was on the Day of Pentecost. The miraculous story is found in Acts 2:1-4:

"And when the day of Pentecost had come, they were all together in one place. And suddenly there came from heaven a noise like a violent, rushing wind, and it filled the whole house where they were sitting. And there appeared to them tongues as of fire distributing themselves, and they rested on each of them. And they were all filled with the Holy Spirit and began to speak with other tongues, as the Spirit was giving them utterance."

Ralph Riggs, an Assemblies of God theologian and a former general superintendent, points to Peter's sermon on the day of Pentecost:

"When Peter preached on the Day of Pentecost, he instructed his audience to repent and be baptized, saying that they then would receive the gift of the Holy Spirit. The Holy Spirit had pricked their hearts. At their repentance He would baptize them into the Body of Christ. They would take a public stand for Christ by being baptized in water in His name. Following that, they would receive the gift of the Holy Spirit. Referring to Acts 2:38, A.J. Gordon says: 'This passage shows logically and chronologically the filling of the Spirit is subsequent to repentance.'"[3]

Most Pentecostals interpret the distinct work of the Holy Spirit baptism as related directly to receiving power for witnessing to others about the saving grace of Christ.

"This baptism in the Spirit is the fulfillment of the promise of the Father which endues men with power from on high.... They were not to depart from Jerusalem until they had received this experience. As glorious as was the good news of salvation wrought by the substitutionary death of Christ on the cross and as urgent as was the need of the proclamation of that gospel, yet they were not even to attempt preaching one sermon or give one testimony until they received this power with which to preach and testify. 'Ye shall receive power, after that the Holy Ghost is come upon you: and ye shall be witnesses unto me' (Acts 1:8, KJV). Power first, and then witnessing. 'Power to witness' is this mighty baptism in the Spirit."[4]

SPEAKING IN OTHER TONGUES

Don and Wesley intensely studied the Book of Acts accounts of the supernatural moving of the Holy Spirit in the first century church. The Nazarene professors at seminary would skirt such issues and suggest that the supernatural manifestation that accompanied the baptism experience in Acts was no longer a pattern for the church. Don and Wesley heard about supernatural acts of the Holy Spirit in revival "hot spots" like Brazil. They knew that if Wesley were ever to receive his healing, it would have to be by a supernatural act of God. They read every book on the subject they could find. Some writers recognized that the baptism in the Holy Spirit was a separate experience but disagreed with the Pentecostals that "speaking in other tongues" was the initial evidence of receiving the baptism.[5]

Speaking in other tongues (sometimes called by its theological name, glossolalia) was a controversial subject within the Holiness Movement from the late nineteenth century on. In the early years of the twentieth century it resulted in the formation of the Pentecostal Movement. It was primarily the tongues issue that set Pentecostal churches apart from other holiness organizations. The Church of the Nazarene was originally called the "Pentecostal Church of the Nazarene" in 1908; but the word "Pentecostal" was deleted from its official name in 1919 to distinguish the Nazarenes from Pentecostals who believed in speaking in tongues.

Pentecostals believe that "speaking in other tongues" is the audible speaking in a language unknown to the speaker that first occurs as an initial evidence of receiving the baptism in the Holy Spirit and continues as a regular experience in the Spirit-filled Christian life. Why do Pentecostals believe this "evidence" or "sign" is necessary? Dr. Stanley Horton explains:

"Only one sign was a part of the Pentecostal baptism. All who were filled with the Holy Spirit began to speak with other tongues as the Spirit gave utterance. That is, they used their tongues, their muscles. They spoke. But the words did not come from their minds or their thinking. The Spirit gave them utterance, which was expressed boldly, loudly, and with obvious anointing and power.... [At Caesarea among the Gentiles] it is clear that a convincing evidence was needed before Peter was willing to say, 'Can any man forbid water, that they would be baptized which have received the Holy Spirit as well as we?' (Acts 10:47, KJV). Something had to show this was the identical gift with that given in Acts 2:4 before the Jerusalem Christians could be satisfied. Peter did not say, 'I hope they received the outpouring, the overflowing experience of Pentecost.' He did not say, 'The Gentiles took it by faith, so I think they have it, I believe they have it.' He knew they were filled, not by their testimony, but by the Holy Spirit's testimony through them. The Spirit gave the evidence, and He gave only one. 'They spoke with tongues and magnified God' (exactly as in Acts 2:4,11). Obviously, speaking in tongues was the convincing evidence here."[6]

Pentecostals point to Acts 10:44-46 to explain the "evidence" issue:

"While Peter was still speaking these words, the Holy Spirit fell upon all those who were listening to the message. And all the circumcised believers who had come with Peter were amazed because the gift of the Holy Spirit had been poured out upon the Gentiles also. For they were hearing them speaking in tongues and exalting God."

THE PENTECOSTAL MOVEMENT

Speaking in other tongues received national attention in religious circles after word spread about a revival in 1901 at Topeka, Kansas, led by Charles Parham, sometimes called the father of the Pentecostal Movement. The Pentecostal revival received even greater attention and criticism when a Parham follower, W.J. Seymour, began a mission on Azusa Street in Los Angeles in 1906. The Los Angeles revival came suddenly as a mighty spiritual whirlwind from heaven:

"The news spread far and wide that Los Angeles was being visited with a 'rushing mighty wind, from heaven'.... One brother states that even before his train entered the city he felt the power of the revival.... Here they find a mighty Pentecostal revival going on from ten o'clock in the morning until about twelve o'clock at night. Pentecost has come to hundreds of hearts. As soon as it is announced that the altar is open for seekers of pardon, sanctification, the baptism in the Holy Ghost, and healing for the body, people rise and flock to the altar. There is no urging.... Coming to the altar, many fall prostrate under the power of God and often come out speaking in tongues."[7]

U. S. GRANT

Don and Wesley kept an open mind on the tongues issue while they were seeking the power of the Holy Spirit. Their quest led them to seek out U.S. Grant, the longtime pastor of First Assembly of God in Kansas City, Kansas. Someone had told Don that Pastor Grant had a history of leading people from non-Pentecostal churches into the baptism in the Holy Spirit.

U.S. Grant was born in Dallas, Texas, on December 30, 1910. He grew up as a member of First Assembly of God in Dallas and was gloriously called to preach at age nineteen. One Sunday night he was wrestling mentally with God about what direction his life would take. He left the church service and waited quietly on the Lord in a small chapel behind the church. A faithful deacon prayed with Grant until the answer came. Grant says that night he felt he had to preach the gospel even if he had to do it from a soapbox. He pastored and pioneered churches in Oklahoma and Texas before taking the senior pastor position in Kansas City, Kansas, in 1946, a position that he would hold for 31 years before his retirement.[8]

Wesley called Pastor Grant's office to set up an appointment for Don and him to learn more about the baptism in the Holy Spirit. They arrived at the church office just after dark. The church didn't have a ramp so Don pulled Wesley in his manual wheelchair up the steps. After finding Brother Grant's office, they knocked with more than just a little anticipation, and he met them at the door. They told him they were Nazarene seminary students and wanted to know more about the baptism. Pastor Grant gave them an overview of church history from the Day of Pentecost to the 20th century. He read Bible passages concerning the baptism in the Holy Spirit and then asked the two eager students, "Are you ready? Do you want this?"

Don and Wesley both said they did.

Pastor Grant moved first to the side of Wesley's wheelchair. As he laid hands on Wesley's head and began to pray, the Holy Spirit fell upon Wesley, and he immediately began speaking in tongues. Pastor Grant moved to the chair where Don was kneeling; and shortly after laying hands on Don's head and praying, Don received the baptism in the Holy Spirit and began speaking in tongues.

For these two young seminarians whose rational faculties were well developed and disciplined, the baptism happened quickly and decisively. It was a moment destined to have far reaching significance in their lives and those of countless others.

When they got back in the car, Don said, "Well, what do you think?"

Wesley responded, "Well, I think your praying in tongues sounded better than mine."

Don looked at Wesley with surprise and said he thought Wesley's speaking in tongues was better than his.

They were silent for a long time during the ride home. They were both Nazarenes. They knew their professors and elders in the Nazarene church would not approve of their actions that night in Pastor Grant's office. They realized that their ministry in the Church of the Nazarene would be over if anyone discovered their secret.

They told no one about their experience.

Don and Wesley subscribed to the *Pentecostal Evangel*, the weekly magazine published by the Assemblies of God, to have some link with Pentecostals. And, when a Pentecostal evangelist or missionary would appear in Kansas City, Don and Wesley would try to attend the service. On one occasion they attended a rally where an assistant to David Wilkerson spoke about Teen Challenge. Don was so excited about this ministry and what the Holy Spirit was doing through it, he rode with the preacher all the way back to Springfield, Missouri, from Kansas City after the service just so he could talk to him at length. After the long night, Don caught a bus back to Kansas City.[9]

WEDDING BELLS

Another important event in Don's life during his seminary years was his marriage to Linda Sodowsky. When Linda completed the first semester of her senior year at Bethany Nazarene College in Oklahoma in January, 1966, she moved to her parents' home in Kansas City to be closer to Don. She enrolled at the University of Missouri at Kansas City to complete the hours necessary for her bachelor's degree. In May, she transferred the hours back to BNC and graduated with her class with a degree in elementary education.

The following month, wedding bells rang for Linda and Don. They were married on June 25, 1966, at First Church of the Nazarene in Kansas City by her father Paul Sodowsky and Pastor William Ellwanger.

That summer Don and Linda moved back to Oklahoma City to live with Don's grandmother; and Don went back to his old concrete finishing job to earn money for the fall semester at seminary. In August, they moved to an apartment in Kansas City. Linda taught second grade for the two years it took Don to complete seminary.[10]

In May, 1968, Wesley and Don graduated from Nazarene Theological Seminary with high honors, magna cum laude, and ranked second and third respectively in their graduating class in grade point average. Wesley went on to earn a Ph.D. with highest honors at Baylor University. Don had the intellect and academic achievements to do the same had that been God's will for his life. But God had a different path for him to walk before these two close friends would join together sixteen years later on a writing project of immense importance and significance for the Pentecostal and Charismatic Movements worldwide.

Both Don and Linda knew God had called them to be missionaries. The Church of the Nazarene had a requirement that missionaries would not be sent out until they had pastored a local church for two years.[11] Don and Linda were ready to go to Brazil immediately after Don's graduation, but they knew they had to find a local church to serve for two years. A friend from BNC days, Calvin Nicholson, recommended Don to the Church of the Nazarene in Goodland, Kansas.

PUSH BACK THE
DARKNESS

❧ *Chapter 7* ❧

Pastors in Goodland

Goodland is about as far west as you can go in Kansas. It is located in Sherman County, named after General William T. Sherman. When the Kansas legislature created the county in 1873, it was part of a vast plain, an unsettled frontier that stretched from central Kansas to the foothills of the Rockies. Many Americans headed west after the Civil War, and farmers found good land in Sherman County to grow their crops.[1]

Goodland was still a town centered around agriculture when Don and Linda arrived in August, 1968, to pastor the Goodland Church of the Nazarene. Range cattle thrived on the nutritious grass, and sorghum grain for winter feed grew well in the Sherman County soil; but wheat was king. Two-thirds of the county's crop-producing acres were in wheat even though corn, sorghum, alfalfa, and sugar beets also were grown.[2]

Even though the land is flat and open, Sherman County is home to many kinds of wildlife. Deer mingle comfortably with the grazing cattle. Small herds of antelope roam the hills. Songbirds and other animals are in abundance. Hunters flock to Sherman County each year during pheasant season.

THE GOODLAND CHURCH

The Goodland Church of the Nazarene, located at Third and Caldwell, was a small congregation of thirty-eight people when Don and Linda arrived as pastors. But the size of the congregation did not discourage them. Don was fresh out of seminary and had a burning desire to preach the gospel. He accepted the challenge and pledged to God that he and Linda would do everything possible to reach the lost in the Goodland area.

Don considered his first day as a pastor in Goodland a disaster. The next day he wrote to Wesley Adams:

"The people are fine. The only thing not good about the service was me. To say the least, I was scared and showed it. I messed up even on the small stuff before preaching, like the announcements and offering. The only good thing was the sermon. I did a pretty good job. Sunday night was just as bad. I goofed up once in the sermon. During prayer Sunday night I left the choir standing and the congregation sitting. My wife about died over that. Anyway, I was sure glad when it was over. I felt like quitting the ministry (at least the pastorate) and I might yet if I don't improve. I visited all the people before Sunday as I planned. I did real well at that. It's about the only thing I did do well...."[3]

Don now knew the reality of what he had been forewarned, namely that his stuttering problem would be a hindrance to his ministry. It frustrated him terribly. If he began stuttering, he slowed down and tried all the tricks he had learned from past therapy.

Don identified with the farmers and ranchers in Sherman County even though he grew up in the city. He loved animals and enjoyed riding around the big western Kansas farms with his parishioners. The people loved Don and Linda. They trusted the tall, straight-talking "Okie." They knew he was sincere in his love for the Lord and in his ambition to take the gospel to everyone in Goodland. Over a two-year period, several families were saved, and two young men were called to preach. Don spent hours at a time sitting on the front porch of a farmhouse and inviting the residents to church on Sunday. He talked their language, he loved their farms and their animals, and he loved their souls. He tried to treat everyone right. Everyone knew exactly where Don stood.

Don reported his successes at soul-winning to Wesley. In late fall of 1969, he wrote:

"I landed two of them last Monday night. One was a young girl about ten or eleven. Her mother wanted me to come over and talk to her. I didn't feel too good about that. It was too easy. Two hours later I met a 61-year-old man who lives down from the church here. So after talking to him for awhile, I asked him his age. He told me. So I said he may not have many more years to live and if he died tonight would he know for sure he would go to heaven. He said no. So I asked him if he would like to know. He said he would. I reached for my Bible, and it wasn't in my pocket. Well I felt kind of stupid, not having my Bible with me. So I told him to wait five minutes and I would run home and get it. I came back and he was still there waiting. I went through the Scriptures with him, and he prayed. He says he's coming to church Sunday. I'll go back Saturday and make sure. I sure would like to get one like that every week."[4]

PRAY MIGHTILY!

Even though Don was taking the gospel to the lost, he couldn't stand the problems he had with stuttering during his sermons. In the same letter to Wesley, Don told his friend how troubled his heart was:

"I suggest you pray extra hard next Sunday. If it continues, I shall give myself three more Sundays. I will assume it is God's will that I leave the pastorate and resign. This will mean also no mission field. From there, I don't know where I will go. I think at the moment I feel much like you. Frustrated because I'm blocked by a handicap. Well, who knows what God is going to do with us? Pray mightily!"

After the next weekend services, Don reported to Wesley by letter:

"You must have not interceded mightily enough for my last Sunday service. It did not go too good. I was real nervous again, stuttered more than usual. I'm trying to analyze the whole thing but can't come to many answers.... I can't remember when I was so embarrassed, humiliated. And then Sunday night was not much better.... This sermon making is a mess. Paul never would have made it if he had had to prepare three dissertations a week and spend 40 hours doing it. I probably spend five to eight hours on each sermon. You must pray 'like all get out' that God will lead me to have one person who will respond. If I can get one or two souls, then I can really go. So pray that God will work."[5]

It was apparent that God did not intend for Don to stop preaching, so He answered prayer and Don's preaching improved dramatically. He still stuttered, but less frequently. He was beginning to feel comfortable in the pulpit, and God continued to bless his ministry with new converts and a growing church.

MINISTRY IN GOODLAND

Loren Rovenstine had arrived in Goodland just a day or two before the Stamps family in 1968. He and his wife Ruth had been called to pastor the local Wesleyan Church. Loren was born in Hutchinson, Kansas, and graduated from Bartlesville Wesleyan College in Bartlesville, Oklahoma, and the Nazarene Theological Seminary in Kansas City. Loren and Don became close friends within weeks of their arrival in Goodland. Don impressed the Rovenstine children, Jeff and Les, by riding a big white horse up to their window at one o'clock in the morning. Don and Loren hunted together, played Rook, and argued theology to the early morning hours. Both were concerned about the liberal trend they saw developing in the Nazarene and Wesleyan churches. Both unconditionally believed in the inerrancy of the Bible. Don became close to Loren's brothers who visited Goodland often. When Loren's father, a retired Wesleyan minister, came to Goodland, Don really took care of him. On one occasion, Don gave the elder Rovenstine $500 that he really didn't have to give. Don said, "God told me to do it, and I did it. That's all there is to it."

Don and Loren joined the Goodland Ministerial Alliance. At the first meeting an Episcopalian minister sat at the other end of the table, blowing smoke rings. They couldn't stand it and joined with several other local pastors in forming their own ministerial group. Don had great respect for most of the pastors in Goodland. He saw in several of them a genuine desire to see lost souls saved. He and Loren would meet several times a month at one of their churches, have communion, and walk around the church, praying for the people of Goodland.[6]

Don's love for practical jokes had not waned with age. He always teased Loren about how boring the missionary films were that Loren showed on Sunday nights in his church. One Sunday night, in the middle of the missionary film, Don went around behind Loren's church and turned off the electricity. Loren had no idea what caused the power outage and dismissed the service. He knew what had really happened when he saw the grin on Don's face the next morning.[7]

REVIVAL SERVICES

In December, 1969, Wesley Adams came to Goodland to hold a week of revival services for Don and Linda Stamps at the Nazarene Church. After graduating from seminary with Don, Wesley had been living at Gaylord, Kansas, and was pastoring the nearby Nazarene Church at Osborne. Don and Wesley had been ordained together as Nazarene ministers in a special service in Wichita in the summer of 1969. Don advertised the Goodland revival services with a special handbill that said:

"Rev. Wesley Adams, of Gaylord, Kansas, will be the evangelist for these services. At the age of sixteen he was severely injured in an auto accident, which resulted in the paralysis of his body. He is wholly committed to God's will and resigned to His providence. He is endeavoring to spend his life in evangelism for Christ."

"Although confined to a wheelchair, Mr. Adams is a forceful speaker and manifests a gracious Christlike spirit. His messages are delivered from an unusual pulpit chair, mechanically operated."[8]

For the revival services, Don also brought to Goodland a well-known recording artist and song evangelist, Paul McNutt from Kansas City.

Wesley had heard Don's story about Brother Jones and his conversion several times, but he had never really understood how remarkable and supernatural Don's conversion had been until during the Goodland revival. The last Sunday morning of the revival a hardened rancher sat through

Wesley's message. Wesley could tell by the expressions on the man's face that strong conviction of the Holy Spirit was on him. The rancher's wife was faithful to the church and had asked Don to pray for her husband many times. During the altar call Don went to where the rancher sat half-way back in the congregation on the inside aisle. When Don touched his elbow, the rancher went to pieces and walked to the altar and wept for an hour. Wesley saw a similarity in the conversion experience of the rancher and Don, and now knew why Don had always wanted his relationship with God to be as powerful as that first night at the Free Will Baptist Church in Oklahoma City.[9]

THEIR FIRST CHILD

While at Goodland, Don and Linda had their first child when Linda gave birth to Toby Don Stamps on June 22, 1969. Linda woke Don up at five o'clock on Sunday morning and told him she was having contractions. They immediately went to the hospital. Fortunately, the district superintendent was already scheduled to preach the morning message. Don stayed with Linda at the hospital all day until Toby came at 5:20 p.m. Don was so excited that he couldn't preach Sunday night. So he had one of the laymen read his sermon that Linda had typed the day before.

Don faced a crisis in his ministry. Linda had always typed his sermons but now was in the hospital with Toby. When Linda's mother came on the train the next Wednesday from Kansas City to help with the baby, Don wouldn't take her to see Linda and Toby until Mrs. Sodowsky had typed his sermon for the Wednesday night service.[10] (As a matter of fact, years later he wrote the notes for *The Full Life Study Bible* with ballpoint pen on yellow legal pads.)

MISSIONARY CANDIDATES

In the fall of 1969 Don and Linda Stamps officially applied for missionary appointment. Even though the church in Goodland was advancing steadily, they knew their call from God was to the mission field. Don knew he was called specifically to Brazil; and Linda was willing to follow wherever her husband was led by God. They made application to Dr. Everett S. Phillips, the executive secretary of the Department of World Missions of the Church of the Nazarene at the church's international headquarters in Kansas City. After preliminary information was obtained, Don and Linda and other missionary candidates met in January, 1970, with the denomination's General Church Board, which approved and appointed missionaries.

The Church of the Nazarene officials decide where its missionaries are assigned. The individual missionary can express his or her desire, but the final decision is made by the missions board. Don told Linda he would not go anywhere but Brazil because God had specifically called him to that country years before. The chance that Don and Linda would be appointed to Brazil looked slim when they appeared before the missions board; that same day Jim and Sally Bond had been appointed to Brazil. What were the chances that another couple would be appointed to Brazil that same day? One hundred percent, because God had called Don Stamps to take the gospel to that land. Sure enough, the missions board approved Don and Linda on January 20, 1970, for assignment in Brazil. They rejoiced all the way back home to Goodland.[11]

In August, 1970, Wesley Adams moved to Waco, Texas, to work on his Ph.D. at Baylor University. During his pastorate at Osborne and Gaylord, Kansas, God spoke to Wesley about being a college teacher. He and Don had continued to believe for Wesley's divine healing. Wesley read Kathryn Kuhlman's book, *God Can Do It Again*, and learned that Kuhlman was coming to a Full Gospel Businessmen's Fellowship convention in Dallas in September. Don drove to Waco from Kansas and took Wesley, Wesley's parents, and former BNC fellow student Jim Dimick to the convention. Wesley again was not healed; but his father was! The elder Adams had been skeptical about Kathryn Kuhlman's ministry, but went to the convention with a severely strained shoulder and left completely healed.[12]

Don struggled with whether or not it was time to leave the church in Goodland. God was blessing the church. It had now grown from thirty-eight to ninety-five in attendance, and God was moving. The church won the "outstanding small church" award in the Kansas District in 1970. Yet, Don and Linda knew God wanted them to be missionaries, so they resigned from the Goodland church. It was hard because they had grown to love the people and the plains of western Kansas.

In the summer of 1970, Linda attended the Nazarene Missions Orientation at Olivet Nazarene College in Kankakee, Illinois. Don had asked permission from the Nazarene officials to attend a special clinic in Toronto, Canada, that had a worldwide reputation for helping people with stuttering problems. Don prayed that this time something could help. The Toronto clinic did wonders for his problem, so that stuttering would never be a major stumbling block for him again. He had learned that sometimes God heals, sometimes He does not, and sometimes He leads His children to the right solution.

95

Don and Linda made their final plans to leave for Brazil. It was hectic filling out dozens of forms to obtain passports and visas. Their dream to become missionaries was coming true. Little did they know that in just fourteen months their missionary careers and their lives would be in shambles.

Don Stamps, age 3. ▶

▲ Woody, Emma, Bobby, David, and Don.

▲ *(l to r) David Brown, Don, John and David Fine.*

▲ *Brother Jones, 1970.*

◀ *Don's high school graduation photo.*

▲ *Lowell Reed (l) and Don were track stars at Putnam City.*

99

▲ Woody and Emma
Stamps, 1993.

▲ Don and Linda were married in 1966.

◄ *The official missionary card, 1971.*

▲ *Todd (l) and Toby, Easter, 1975.*

101

▲ *Don and Jim Dimick, 1976.*

▲ *On the farm in western Kansas, 1982.*

◄ *The Don Stamps family, 1979.*

▲ *Bob Silkman (l) became Don's farming mentor.*

▼ *In the mountains of Brazil, 1981.*

▼ *Tiffany, 1982.*

▼ *Don, Toby, and Todd enjoyed riding their horses.*

▼ *Don Stamps loved his kids.*

◄ *Don always loved fishing. This big catch came from the Pantanal area of Brazil.*

▼ *A Prayer cave at Prayer Mountain in South Korea.*

Don preaching to a full house at Campinas Assembly of God, 1983.

▲ Don preaches to thousands along the seashore in the northeastern Brazilian state of Alagoas, 1985. Almost 500 were baptized in the Atlantic Ocean at the end of the service.

▲ Don and Brazillian Assemblies of God pastors and workers, 1983.

▼ *Don and missionary Dave Harrison, literally up a tree.*

▲ *Brazil, 1981. (l to r) Bob Combs, Mark Lemos, and Don.*

▲ *(l to r) Dan Davis, Don, Lawrence Williams, 1984.*

▲ *Missionary Randall Walker and Don in Brazil.*

▲ *Don spent thousands of hours of study in writing the notes for* The Full Life Study Bible.

113

▼ Dr. Stanley Horton (l) was the Chairman of the FLSB editorial commitee.

▲ Many of the notes for the FLSB were written on the front porch of the Stamps home in Brazil.

▲ *Don and associate editor of the FLSB, Wesley Adams.*

115

▲ *Rev. Loren Triplett, Executive Director of the Division of Foreign Missions of the Assemblies of God, introduces the FLSB and the Stamps family.*

▲ Oklahoma Assemblies of God District Superintendent
Armon Newburn stands in front of the stone world map
presented to Oklahoma by the Stamps family.

◀ *Don and Linda Stamps, 1990.*

▲ *The Stamps family, 1988.*

PUSH BACK THE DARKNESS

❦ *Chapter 8* ❧

The Problem in Brazil

*T*he young missionary family arrived in Campinas, Brazil, on January 9, 1971, after a twenty-four-hour flight from Oklahoma City. They were excited and yet apprehensive. This was a new country, a new culture, a new language. Linda had 18-month-old Toby to care for in a strange land, and she was pregnant again. Don later recalled his feelings:

"I was sad to leave our loved ones but so glad to see that plane lift off. We were finally going to the field. We got to Brazil, and I stepped off the plane and was finally a missionary! If someone would have walked up to me and handed me a ten-million-dollar check and said go back home, I would have torn it up. This is all I ever wanted in life."[1]

MISSION FIELD: BRAZIL

Brazil is larger than the continental United States. The vast country occupies more than half of the South American continent. It was originally inhabited by Indian tribes until Portugal colonized the land around 1534. The early explorers called it Brazil because of the red dyewood (brazilwood) discovered there. When sugar became a major crop, millions of African slaves were imported to work in the fields. The discovery of diamonds and gold in the seventeenth and eighteenth centuries brought hundreds of thousands of Portuguese who began developing the tropical interior of the country. Brazil became an independent republic in 1889.

The 158 million people of Brazil constitute a melting pot of races and cultures. About sixty percent of the people trace their ancestry to Europe. There are large groups of Italians, Portuguese, Germans, and Spaniards. A fourth of the population is a mixture of black, Indian, and European ancestry. About ten percent are black. Less than one percent are of Indian blood.

Farmers in Brazil are among the world leaders in production of food. Coffee, sugar, and soybeans join with iron ore to lead their annual export list. About one-fourth of Brazil's trade is with the United States.

Brazil consists of twenty-two states, four territories, and the federal district of Brasilia, the nation's capital.[2]

Campinas is a city of about one million people located eighty miles northwest of Sao Paulo in the southeastern state of Sao Paulo. It is located in what is called "the heartland" of Brazil. The Central and Southern Plateaus contain the most fertile lands, largest cities, richest mines, and half of Brazil's population. Temperatures range from 50 to 99 degrees Fahrenheit, and the southern-hemisphere Brazilian winter is from June to September.

Eighty-five percent of Brazilians are Roman Catholic. Monks and priests came with early Portuguese explorers and evangelized the Indians. Brazil was the first country in South America influenced by Protestants. The German Lutherans and Presbyterians sent missionaries in the late 1800's and other Protestants, including Pentecostals, came early in the 20th century.

NAZARENE MISSIONARIES

The Church of the Nazarene had planted 19 churches in southern Brazil in the thirteen years before Don and Linda arrived. Earl Mosteller was the pioneer missionary who began the Nazarene effort in 1958. Until 1971, he was the Brazil field superintendent and directed the Nazarene missionaries in the country.

Don, Linda, and the young Toby stayed with the Mostellers for the first two weeks in Campinas before they moved into their own house on a busy street in the city. Tragedy almost struck the young family when Toby was chasing a dog and followed it into the path of a van. The driver was able to slow down substantially, but Toby's head was struck by the van's right headlight. Miraculously, Toby suffered only minor cuts and bruises. However, Don quickly decided to move to the country.

They found a small acreage, called a *chacara*, in the countryside outside Campinas. The foliage in the area was beautiful. Poinsettias, avocados, and bananas grew in their back yard. Toby had a collie puppy named Kansas, so named for the good memories Don and Linda had from living in Goodland. Toby had outgrown his baldness and now had lots of curly blond hair. Don was able to buy a small car the second week in Brazil. Nazarenes in the Kansas District and offerings from friends made it possible to buy a Ford Corcel. Linda was getting settled and wrote home:

"I am enjoying Brazil and getting used to being a Brazilian housewife. Getting fruits, vegetables, and meat from the open market is quite different, but they are delicious. The homes are different, especially the kitchens, but I'm enjoying making our house into a home. To the Brazilians I am Dona Linda. That is their way of saying Mrs. Linda. Women are always called by their first names. I am feeling fine and am looking forward to the arrival of the new baby in June."[3]

Don and Linda became close to two other Nazarene missionary couples: Roger and Mary Maze and Jim and Sally Bond.

Roger and Mary, from Ohio, had been in Brazil since 1964. Roger had been encouraged by his family and his teachers at school to be a lawyer; but one night at age seventeen he had a dream. He was in a chapel and a missionary was preaching and saying that she was going to retire and someone in the service would take her place. In the dream Roger went forward, and she laid her hands on him. Roger immediately awoke. All self-will was gone, and the presence of God was powerful. In the following days, God revealed that Roger would be a missionary somewhere in the western hemisphere. He graduated from Malone College in Canton, Ohio, the Nazarene Theological Seminary in Kansas City, and studied anthropology and linguistics at the Hartford Seminary Foundation (formerly the Kennedy School of Missions) in Hartford, Connecticut. While working with the Cree Indians in northern Alberta, Canada, God spoke to Roger about Brazil. The Nazarene missions board agreed with his call.

In the years before Don arrived, Roger and Mary pastored a church in Belo Horizonte in the mountains of southeastern Brazil north of Rio de Janeiro and taught in the branch Bible college there. After spending 1968 back in America to obtain a master's degree at Northwestern University and Garrett Theological Seminary, Roger returned to Brazil as the interim field superintendent for missions.[4]

Jim and Sally Bond arrived in Campinas about three weeks after Don and Linda. They had been approved by the Nazarene missions board at the same time Don and Linda were approved. Jim is a third-generation Nazarene. By age fifteen he knew God had placed a special call on his life. He was an outstanding athlete in high school and was offered an athletic scholarship by several colleges around the country. He signed a letter of intent to play basketball at Texas A & M. However, at the last moment before entering college, he changed his mind. Or, God changed Jim's mind, and he enrolled at Pasadena College—now Point Loma Nazarene College in San Diego, California, where Jim now serves as college president.

Before they accepted their appointment to Brazil, Jim and Sally pastored at Olathe, Kansas; Casper, Wyoming; and Nampa, Idaho. Jim was not content pastoring in America after discovering that only six percent of those involved in ministry as a vocation were working with the ninety-one percent of the world's population that was non-English speaking. Acknowledging the injustice of such imbalance, he made himself available to the Nazarene missions board in Kansas City. He was serving on the general board of the Nazarenes and had the opportunity to vote with the other members of that board to send himself and Sally to Brazil.

Jim Bond recalls his first weeks on the mission field and his contact with Don:

"Don was consumed by his desire to evangelize. When we first got to Brazil, all Don could talk about was wanting to form a partnership with the Spirit and evangelize Brazil. He had the spiritual intensity and evangelistic fervor of the primitive church. He was intolerant, stubborn, a little narrow, but very intense. He was one of God's unique people."[5]

It was the custom for Nazarene missionaries to spend their first year on assignment in language school to become accustomed to the new language and the unfamiliar culture before they were given a full-time assignment. On March 1, Don and Linda and Jim and Sally began the nine-month language school. They found the Brazilian people very friendly, patient, and helpful as they tried to communicate with them. Don wrote Wesley Adams on March 1:

"I just finished my first day of language school. I think it will be pretty good. They concentrate a lot in language study related to pronunciation. For the first two weeks we do nothing but say words and sentences that we do not know the meaning of. They have been taking me around to the different churches and having me give my testimony. The Lord seems to bless it every time.... I talked to Mosteller yesterday. He told me after I finish language school he would let me go off and try any method I want.

"My method of course will be, at all costs, get the converted truly baptized in the Holy Spirit. If I can accomplish that, the thing will go. If not, very little fruit will be gained.... I wish the Lord would just heal you and you could come down here and together we would get something started."[6]

THE PROBLEM WITH TONGUES

After their very first night in Brazil, Don told Linda, "There's a problem here. I don't know what it is, but there's definitely a problem." Just two weeks later, it surfaced. About half of the Nazarene national pastors in Brazil had received the baptism in the Holy Spirit and were speaking in tongues, at least in the privacy of their prayer closets. In four of the nineteen Nazarene organized churches, there were occasional outbreaks of speaking in tongues during services.

The problem arose when Field Superintendent Earl Mosteller and other Nazarene missionaries had to decide whether to ordain the national pastors who admitted speaking in tongues.[7]

The "Holy Spirit problem" had first arisen in the Nazarene churches a few years before during Roger Maze's first term. Dr. Mosteller had even asked Roger to write his master's thesis on the subject at Garrett Theological Seminary. Many of the national pastors and church leaders in the Nazarene churches in Brazil came from a background in Pentecost and accepted the baptism in the Holy Spirit and speaking in tongues as part of their Christian experience. By 1971, eight out of ten evangelical believers in Brazil were Pentecostal.

Don, Roger, and Jim were "middle of the road" in their interpretation of "speaking in tongues." True to their Nazarene training, they did not believe that tongues was the exclusive initial evidence of receiving the baptism but felt that tongues, being included in the scriptural lists of spiritual gifts, must be acknowledged and that its use should be in harmony with the guidelines laid down by Paul in 1 Corinthians 14:

"Pursue love, yet desire earnestly spiritual gifts, but especially that you may prophesy. For one who speaks in a tongue does not speak to men, but to God; for no one understands, but in his spirit he speaks mysteries. But one who prophesies speaks to men for edification and exhortation and consolation. One who speaks in a tongue edifies himself; but one who prophesies edifies the church. Now I wish that you all spoke in tongues, but even more that you would prophesy; and greater is one who prophesies than one who speaks in tongues, unless he interprets, so that the church may receive edifying" (verses 1-5).

Paul went on to say in the same passage:

"If anyone speaks in a tongue [addressing the congregation], it should be by two or at the most three, and each in turn, and let one interpret; but if there is no interpreter, let him keep silent in the church; and let him speak to himself and to God.... Therefore, my brethren, desire earnestly to prophesy, and do not forbid to speak in tongues. But let all things be done properly and in an orderly manner" (verses 27-39).

Frankly, by 1971, many Nazarene ministers and theologians had adopted the stance of moderation on the issue. The official doctrinal statements in the church's manual did not address the issue clearly. The unofficial prohibition of tongues by the denomination was articulated by three well-known Nazarene authors: Donald S. Metz, *Speaking in Tongues*; B.F. Neely, *The Bible Versus the Tongues Theory*; and W.T. Purkiser, *Spiritual Gifts: Healing and Tongues*.

The "tongues problem" that arose in Brazil would echo all the way to Kansas City and cause the denomination's leaders in the next few years to take an official position against speaking in tongues.

Dr. Mosteller, the field superintendent in Brazil, began asking the missionaries their positions. He was disturbed that most of the Nazarene missionaries under his leadership did not see a problem with the national pastors speaking in tongues in private as long as it did not cause disorder or difficulties in the local church. Don revealed to Dr. Mosteller and Roger Maze that he had received the baptism back in Kansas City during seminary and spoke in tongues. Linda, however, still did not know. She had never known that Don had sought the baptism, much less received it. She had been raised as a strict Nazarene and had been taught that speaking in tongues was not of God.[8]

THE OFFICIAL POSITION

Dr. Mosteller needed an answer to the dilemma over ordination of the national pastors. He wrote to Dr. V.H. Lewis, one of the six general superintendents of the Church of the Nazarene in Kansas City, for guidance. Dr. Mosteller did not think the pastors who spoke in tongues should be ordained, but he wanted harmony among his missionaries and openly discussed the problem. Dr. Lewis was the general superintendent with jurisdiction over the part of the globe that included Brazil. His response to Dr. Mosteller in April was straight and to the point:

"We will not ordain any tongues-speaking candidate or men who believe in speaking in tongues, whether they have gone through what they claim is that experience or not, and this I am sure would hold in any area of the church. So you can proceed with authority along that line."[9]

Don wrote to Wesley on April 17:

"I couldn't believe it. No one can even believe in tongues! Roger Maze said even he couldn't be ordained under these rules. Well, none of us cared for this ruling except Mosteller. Jim Bond even said if he, Lewis, means what he said, he will have to turn in his papers. The position of Larry Clark [another Nazarene missionary] is more like Mosteller's but not as radical. So he's safe. Roger is very upset, of course. Bob Collins [another missionary] doesn't like it and is somewhat confused.

"I am, as you may expect, quite disturbed, angry, and vocal. I let Mosteller know what I thought of such an incompetent statement. For about three hours last night, we met with him. Roger did well in the meeting. Mosteller's reaction to us is very mild. He knows he has an explosive case on his hands and is outnumbered five to one. Regardless

of consequences, I am going to have Roger take me to see
Bernhard Johnson of the Assemblies of God and see what
the possibilities are of getting in with them in Brazil. This is
what I want you to pray about hard. Pray for the Lord's will
to be done. Either open the way or close it. Roger knows
Johnson personally."[10]

THE MISSIONARIES' RESPONSE

Don felt the prohibition against ordaining national pastors who spoke in tongues also had ramifications for Nazarene
missionaries who at least accepted the fact that a legitimate
gift of tongues could exist. The missionaries wanted to write
Dr. Lewis for a clarification of his letter. Dr. Mosteller said it
was very clear what Lewis meant. When the missionaries
remarked that they all might have to leave also, Dr. Mosteller
relayed that fear to Dr. Lewis. He requested a letter outlining
the position of those who opposed him. Don wrote the letter
but senior missionaries Roger Maze and Bob Collins signed
the five-page letter sent to Dr. Lewis in early May:

"We are writing this letter because of the confusion and
misunderstanding.... It is our hope that by this letter you
might better understand our position and have added insight
into the situation which may help in the formation of a policy relative to Brazil.... No missionary has ever threatened to
leave the field or the church because of the policy you suggested. However, we did feel that the implications of that
policy put our missionary relationship in jeopardy....

"Secondly, we are just as interested as you in not aban-
doning the Church of the Nazarene in Brazil to the
Pentecostal Movement.... We believe the Church of the
Nazarene has a distinctive doctrine to proclaim, namely the

experience of cleansing from all sin through the blood of Christ....

"With regard to the speaking in tongues in the congregation, it is still a minority affair. Out of about nineteen churches, we have only four where speaking in tongues during a public service might occur. However, we did determine at our last meeting with the pastors that fourteen of the nineteen felt that there is a possibility of a valid gift of tongues...."[11]

Don's letter pointed out that *The Beacon Bible Commentary*, published by the Beacon Hill Press (same as the Nazarene Publishing House), recognized "there was a valid gift of languages in the early church" (XIII,431). In the discussion of spiritual gifts on the same page, the commentary recognizes "the true Pentecostal gift of speaking in unknown languages" and also "the kind of tongues that were known in Corinth." On page 452 of the commentary, the gift of tongues is believed to be "some utterance not in the commonly understood language." On page 455, it said of tongues that "this gift was not to be forbidden or despised. For in its own place and in its proper time it may be a valuable endowment."

The letter to Dr. Lewis continued:

"In fairness to the writer of our commentary on 1 Corinthians, Dr. Metz, we would say that we understand that his work was edited and that his position is somewhat different than what is presented in the commentary. However, what should be pointed out is that the editorial committee has taken what can be called 'a middle road position,' and this is essentially what the majority of our pastors believe. We feel that it would be discriminatory to take punitive measures against our pastors (fourteen of them) for taking this position and at the same time allow the editorial committee, several pastors and missionaries, some general leaders, and not a few seminary and college professors, to maintain an identical solution....

"A possible solution, and one presented by Dr. Metz in his book *Speaking in Tongues*, is the one that we feel should be taken.... We feel that what Dr. Metz says on page 88 is wise. He states: 'Don't quarrel about tongues, don't make it an issue of division, but seek to proclaim God's Word'.... Dr. Metz feels that if Paul had taken a very hard line that there would have been quarreling about tongues and divisions. Probably the same would happen on the field if another approach is taken other than what Paul delineates....

"We feel that with these restrictions (outlined by Paul in 1 Corinthians) alongside the teaching of the relative unimportance of tongues compared to other gifts, the Church of the Nazarene in Brazil would concentrate on being what God wants it to be and move on to accomplish God's purpose here.... This is the position that we feel would be the wisest to take with our people in Brazil. These are nationals whom we have come to love. They are God's children. Some are misguided and at times confused. What they need is love, understanding, and better teaching upon this subject and many others...."[12]

THE OFFICIAL VISIT

The crisis was put on hold until Dr. Lewis could schedule a trip to Brazil and the problem be presented to the Board of General Superintendents in Kansas City. Jim and Sally Bond and Don and Linda's efforts in language school were severely crippled because they realized their tenure in Brazil could be brief. Don dropped out of language school. Dr. Mosteller knew he had several general leaders behind his stand and was very firm on the issue. Don was frustrated:

"By this time, most of us felt we were fighting for a lost cause. However, I didn't prepare ten years for missionary service just to go home in ten months."[13]

Roger Maze suggested that headquarters send two of the best Nazarene scholars to Brazil to spend a week in prayer and fasting with the Nazarene pastors and missionaries and discuss every passage on tongues in the Bible and try to reach a consensus of opinion. The suggestion received no response from Kansas City.[14]

During all of the turmoil, another curly-headed Stamps child arrived. Todd Jason Stamps was born in Campinas on June 11, 1971.

Wesley Adams encouraged Don to stand for his beliefs on tongues:

"The Nazarene denomination desperately needs a voice to articulate the charismatic position in the light of biblical and contemporary evidence. I believe the issue is ripe for such a voice to be heard in the Nazarene movement. Here's the bombshell! God may be wanting to use you, Don, to be that voice.... It seems providential to me that you would be placed on the same field in the same town as Roger Maze who is of like faith.... On most fields you would have to stand alone.... Perhaps God is looking, seeking, searching for a man through whom He can speak and break down the walls of prejudice so that the Holy Spirit can break out among Nazarenes. Maybe you shouldn't leave the denomination until you've used your influence to the maximum in making the church and its leaders face this issue squarely and openly. Should you lose the fight, I'm sure you would have a hero's welcome in the Charismatic Movement."[15]

135

The severity of the problem deepened among the Nazarene missionary force when former general superintendent, Dr. G.B. Williamson, came to Brazil. He agreed with the policy from headquarters and strongly encouraged the missionaries to be loyal to the denomination and to accept the position taken by the leaders. Dr. Williamson said the missionaries should make up their minds. If they could not follow the edict from their leaders, they should probably return to the States.

In October, Dr. Mosteller was not reelected as field chairman by the other missionaries. However, no one was elected to fill the position since a two-thirds majority was required and no missionary was willing to vote for himself to replace Mosteller. Don and Jim Bond did not vote because they had been on the field for less than two years.

Dr. Lewis sent word he would arrive in Brazil in November to bring the official word on the tongues problem from the church's headquarters in Kansas City. Don was searching for answers. He kept up his contact with the Assemblies of God just to "keep the channels open." Assemblies of God missionaries were favorable to Don who felt he may not "fit in any church exactly."[16]

On November 6, Don wrote a long letter to his seminary missions professor, Dr. Paul Orjala, who had taken a leave of absence from the seminary in Kansas City and was teaching at the Nazarene European Bible College in Switzerland:

"Dr. Lewis comes November the 16th to bring the policy. If it is any other approach than biblical, I do not think the missionaries will accept it. I know I cannot. God's Word is my final authority.... The three older missionaries will probably serve out their terms and go home, never to return again. Jim and I will either be sent home or to an English-speaking field to serve out our terms.

"I talk to Jim a lot.... He is sick of the whole mission program and would prefer to go home and forget the whole thing.... You cannot imagine what this has done to our spirits and zeal for the mission work. It has literally been torn to shreds."[17]

Dr. Lewis came and brought a hard-line position that the church would not ordain any tongues-speaking candidate or anyone who propagates tongues. Furthermore, anyone who propagated tongues would be considered as one who inveighs against the doctrines and usages of the Church of the Nazarene. Dr. Lewis told the missionaries that if they believed in the possibility of tongues, they could be viewed as a potential liability to the policy and work of the church in Brazil. He said if they could not live with the policy, he would help them go home in dignity.

After the first day's meeting with Dr. Lewis, each of the missionaries talked to him privately. Don and Roger Maze told Dr. Lewis they could not live with the policy. Jim Bond told Dr. Lewis that he would accept the policy and articulate it as the church's, but could not in good conscience be a part of enforcing it. Furthermore, Jim maintained that he at least be allowed to state his personal beliefs on the subject when asked. The most objectionable part of the headquarters plan was the requirement that national pastors sign a letter renouncing their Pentecostal experience in the baptism and promising not to speak in tongues in public or in private.[18]

Dr. Lewis was unwavering in his stand on the official position of the church but seemed genuinely concerned about the welfare of his young missionaries.

Don continued in his letter to Dr. Orjala:

"Jim and I are a special problem. Dr. Lewis does not want to send us home at this time because it may cause a bigger problem than anybody wants because of questions that will be asked. Jim and I definitely do not want to stay here in Brazil and ride out our service for three more years when we do not know the language well and will have no motivation to acquire it in any proficient way.... Dr. Lewis has said he would gladly transfer me to another field.... But right now I have no energy to go through another year of language study...and then what if the problem would come up in that field also? I would have to leave there. Dr. Lewis has said he would recommend me anywhere in the States to serve our church, but in Brazil where the tongues problem is so acute, I should not serve. My feelings now are that I have lost my missionary ministry. What I have held as most precious for the last 15 years is gone."[19]

Dr. Lewis spent four days with Don and the other missionaries trying to talk them out of leaving Brazil. Don reflected on these meetings in the letter to Dr. Orjala:

"In all the meetings, Dr. Lewis has been kind. He has tried to convince me...to go off to some city in Brazil where I won't be faced with the issue.... This is Brazil, and 80 percent of all Christians are Pentecostal. There is no place I can go where the issue will not occur. Dr. Lewis has suggested the possibility of me going to teach at the Central American Bible School in Costa Rica or even to the Spanish Bible School in San Antonio, Texas."[20]

Linda's parents were very upset that she and Don were returning from the mission field. However, Dr. Ralph Earle, a distinguished professor at the Nazarene Theological Seminary and a highly respected member of the New International Version translation committee, talked to

Rev. Sodowsky about the problem. Dr. Earle and many seminary professors took a moderate stance on tongues like the position taken by Don and a majority of the Nazarene missionaries in Brazil.[21]

Jim Bond wanted to stay in Brazil if he could. He wrote:

"I spent much time thinking and praying and retreated for a week to our campgrounds just out of Campinas. I reached the conclusion that: (1) I had to be true to myself, pricing a clear conscience above all; (2) I had to be true to God's Word as the Spirit interpreted it to me, regardless of what it cost; (3) I had to be true to my call to preach. I told Dr. Everett Phillips [Nazarene missions executive secretary] I wanted to stay and would respect the position of the church as long as I could also state my personal belief."[22]

Dr. Phillips could not make such a concession, and the Bonds came home in May. They pastored in Oklahoma City and Colorado Springs. Eventually Jim accepted an administrative position at Point Loma Nazarene College. He was elected president in August, 1983, and continues to serve in that capacity. Roger Maze served out his term and did not return to Brazil. He has pastored churches in the north central and southeastern parts of the United States.[23]

GOING HOME

In January, 1972, Don made it official. He was leaving Brazil. In a letter he sent to Dr. Phillips, Don said:

"This is why I am leaving the Brazilian field. What decisions I have made have been because I felt I must be loyal to God's Word as I understand it, even if it costs me the ministry I have prepared ten years for. I decided long before this situation arose that God's Word is my final authority."[24]

Dr. Phillips was given Don's letter while attending a conference in Argentina. He sent Don a handwritten response on stationery of the Plaza Hotel in Buenos Aires:

"Jim gave me your letter, and I have read it with interest and concern. I'm sorry for the developments on the field. So all we can do now is to work toward the best solution possible.... We want what is best for you and Linda, and will abide by any decision you make and stand behind you in that decision."[25]

Dr. Phillips talked about several options, but Don had made up his mind. He was finished in Brazil with the Nazarenes. He wrote to Wesley of his innermost disappointments and frustrations:

"I have decided not to accept any other field. I am coming home."[26]

During the weeks of disappointment after Don and Linda returned from Brazil, Linda's mother prayed for them more fervently than ever before. Kathleen Sodowsky did not understand why the problem in Brazil had happened; but one day during her prayer time God spoke to her in an almost audible voice, saying, "I have something better for them." In the following years Don and Linda would go through many trials and frustrations before God showed them the "something better."

PUSH BACK THE
DARKNESS

Chapter 9

The Desert
Experience

*M*oses, John the Baptist, and Jesus himself had their desert experiences that prepared them for their greatest spiritual work. After Jesus had been forty days in the wilderness being tempted by the devil, He "returned to Galilee in the power of the Spirit" (Luke 4:14).

No man or woman of God enjoys such a time nor does he or she often recognize the significance of the period of suffering except in retrospect; but without humiliation there can be no exaltation. As Jesus' crucifixion had to precede His resurrection; so for Don and Linda Stamps the loss of their dreams, the destruction of their illusions, and a time of seeming to be on the shelf had to occur before they were ready for their greatest challenge.

BACK TO WESTERN KANSAS

In March, 1972, Don, Linda, and the two boys arrived in Oklahoma City. When Don realized that his missionary career might be over, he sat down and cried like a baby. The previous fourteen months of turmoil in Brazil had almost taken his desire for missions from him; and his heart was filled with many questions.

Linda, too, was deeply puzzled. She still did not know that Don had received the baptism in the Holy Spirit and did not fully understand why he had taken such a strong stand in favor of allowing the ordination of tongues-speaking Brazilian pastors. Yet she faithfully supported her husband.

They spent the next five months with Don's parents in Oklahoma City trying to decide between attempts by Nazarene officials to place him in a local church or send him to another mission field. To this day, it seems incredible that the church that rejected them for Brazil would offer to place them as pastors in a church or missionaries in a different country. As the hurt of the departure from Brazil eased, Don and Linda prayed for direction from God. They still felt the Lord had plans for them in Brazil, but they did not know how or when. Don called Wesley Adams, who was still attending Baylor University in Waco, Texas, and told him that he felt alienated from the Nazarenes but that his passion and vision for Brazil was still in his heart.

Don was concerned how he was going to support his family while yet earning enough money to return to Brazil as an independent missionary. He and Linda had enjoyed living and pastoring in Goodland, so they contacted friends in the area. Don loved farming and raising animals and explored the possibility of moving back to Goodland and investing in a farm to make the necessary money to get back to Brazil. After all, beef prices were up, sugar beet prices were up, wheat prices were up. Don sat down with his calculator and figured that he could earn enough in three years to get him back to Brazil.[1]

DON THE FARMER

The Stamps had returned to America with only $2,500 to last them until Don could find some means of support. In August they moved to a $50-a-month farmhouse outside Goodland, Kansas. Here was a city boy with visions of getting rich on the farm. Don decided to raise cattle. He thought he could buy them for $50 each and sell them a few months later for $100 each. He began buying parcels of land on which to pasture the cattle. He contracted to buy eighty calves from Wisconsin. The price was right, but the timing was wrong. The two semis transporting the calves arrived at midnight in a blinding snowstorm. Within two weeks, thirty-five of the calves died of pneumonia, although the surviving calves flourished. However, the bottom fell out of the cattle market about the time the calves were ready to sell. The ledger on Don's cattle-baron project at the end of the year showed a $15,000 loss. In Don's mind, the death of the calves and the major loss was but a temporary setback; he would try pig farming.

He bought four sows and one boar. His trusty calculator told him he could make thousands of dollars a year off of a few "mama" pigs. Sure enough, a few weeks later one of the sows had twelve beautiful piglets. After church on Sunday night Don went out to the barn to check on the baby pigs, and they had all frozen to death. Pig farming was not working out.[2]

Don decided to get him a tractor. Unfortunately, he bought the worst one in town, for it broke down at least once a week. He had it three weeks and broke the axle. It cost $400 to repair. A few weeks later it cost another $400 for repairs. Then the transmission went out, which cost another $800. Don drove the tractor too close to some water, lost control, and drove it into the lake. Yet, he was optimistic about his chances to make it big as a farmer and kept convincing the local banker to loan him more operating capital.[3]

For Linda, life on the farm was a mixed blessing. She enjoyed being a housewife and mother and was at peace, even though the old rental house smelled bad and wind whistled around the windows. Life was tough. They only had $1,500 to live on during the first winter.[4]

As a farmer and rancher, Don spent a lot of time by himself. There was a constant battle in his mind. He asked himself a thousand times if he had made the right decision in Brazil. He questioned God about the call upon his life, why the Brazil problem had occurred, and why a city boy was trying to make a living on a farm in the plains of western Kansas.

He concluded that he had been right to stand up for the inerrancy of the Bible. He thought, "If I'm going to waste my life, I'd rather waste it for God if that means keeping His Holy Word than to have the greatest ministry in the world."[5]

FRIENDS AND FAILURES

Life on the farm would have been unbearable for Don except for the enjoyment he derived from his family and the close companionship of friends. Loren Rovenstine was still pastoring the Goodland Wesleyan Church. Don and Linda didn't feel comfortable attending the Nazarene church they had pastored before going to Brazil, so they worshiped in the Wesleyan church. Loren Rovenstine stood by Don and prayed and counseled with him many times. They would go fishing and talk for hours.[6]

Don deeply desired to do something for God. He longed for Brazil. He didn't know exactly what to do. He continued to follow the progress of the Assemblies of God revival in Brazil and wondered out loud to Pastor Rovenstine if he should contact the Assemblies of God about the possibility of working with them in Brazil.

146

God brought Don and Linda into contact with Bob and Irma Silkman in Goodland. The Silkmans lived in town but farmed hundreds of acres. Bob had been converted only the year before, so they needed each other. Don knew a lot about God and the Bible, and Bob knew a lot about farming. They fished together, worked on each other's farms, and fed cattle in the winter together. Don's influence on Bob's Christian walk was profound.[7]

Don had seen many of his friends make big money on wheat, so he decided to look for a larger parcel of land for a wheat crop. He bought 460 acres at a great price just down the road. Don and his family moved into a somewhat larger farmhouse on the newly purchased land after having lived for a year and a half in the smelly rental house.

The wheat was planted. The rains came, and the wheat grew. Don predicted he could harvest forty bushels per acre. The heads were full just before harvest late one afternoon when a dark cloud loomed on the western horizon. Don and Linda stood in their garage as a massive hailstorm destroyed every acre of wheat. They had no crop insurance and now owed the bank an even more enormous debt.

Cattle prices were rising, and Don convinced the banker to loan him another $40,000 to buy seventy-five cows. A year later the cattle market dipped again. The cows for which he had paid $465 each now sold for $220.

And then, Linda was pregnant again. This time it was different than with her two boys, and she wondered if this one would be a girl.[8]

THE DARKEST HOUR

Although Don was happy about the coming child, his frustrations mounted. The failure at farming was the hardest thing he had ever been through. He became overwhelmed with the thought that he had possibly grieved God and that his punishment was being forsaken, in failure, on the farm. On a visit to see Wesley at Waco, his friend saw the deep disappointment and depression Don was suffering and was afraid Don might lose his faith in God. Wesley spent hours each week praying for Don and Linda. This was the dark night of Don's soul. It was as if God was totally silent and far away. The night would get even darker.

Don often sent Wesley a cassette tape that revealed his innermost thoughts. The tapes are gone but Wesley kept notes he made while listening to the weekly, gloomy report from western Kansas. He told Don:

"Satan is fighting diligently everything you are about because it is a future threat to his kingdom. God is putting you through a trial of faith to enlarge you through pressure; you will eventually come through successfully according to His timing, not yours, when you've learned the spiritual lessons He desires to teach you through this. God trains men in a time of brokenness in order to use them. You are in God's permissive will out there on the farm, but not in His ultimate will."[9]

Wesley compared Don's trials and tribulations with the life of Peter. God took Peter through some very difficult situations in order to make him the man of God He could use fully. Peter experienced tremendous failure. Wesley saw Don going through the same type of suffering and brokenness.

Sugar beets were selling for $45 a ton in 1976. Don decided to devote every acre he owned to sugar beets. The beets produced more than two tons per acre, but by the time of harvest the price had dropped to $18 a ton. Don's optimism turned to gloom and depression.

The bank debt had mushroomed to more than $100,000. Don and Linda began custom farm work. Even though Linda was pregnant again, they drove tractors and trucks, cut wheat, and harvested pinto beans and corn for other farmers in the area. Their days began long before daylight, and they were fortunate to get in bed by midnight. God blessed their efforts, and they paid back almost $70,000 of the bank loan from their earnings in custom farming.

Tiffany Dawn Stamps was born in Goodland on December 4, 1976. The two brothers now had a baby sister who was a delight to the entire family.

THE DARK BEFORE THE DAWN

The custom farming had eased the debt load Don was under, and the spring of 1977 brought new hopes for his vision of extra money to put aside for the return to Brazil. All the neighbors planted alfalfa and corn because prices on those crops were up again. Don's alfalfa was beautiful and green when another hail storm swept across Goodland wiping out their crops and damaging the roof of their house.

Don was now at the low point of his life. Satan told him, "Look at yourself. You were called to be a missionary and a preacher. Look at yourself. God has left you, and He doesn't love you. You are no longer His child. It is all finished."

Linda had to be the strong member of the team. She encouraged Don and prayed for him and with him constantly. Don did not lose his faith completely, but he was feeling devastated and without hope.

One morning during his prayer time, suddenly God gave Don a Scripture verse: "Then I will make up to you for the years that the swarming locust has eaten" (Joel 2:25).

149

Don believed God but began asking, "When, God, when?"

Within a few days God again spoke to Don one morning while he was reading the Bible. God clearly said, "Don, this thing is over. This trial, this test is over and finished."

Jesus, who had seemed so far off for so long, was again close to Don's heart. Later that morning Don was feeding his hogs when God told him to look up that Assemblies of God preacher in Kansas City who had led him and Wesley to the baptism experience more than a decade before.[10]

For the first time in five years Don saw a glimmer of hope for returning to Brazil.

PUSH BACK THE
DARKNESS

Chapter 10

The Long
Road Back

*I*t has always been true that every great man or woman of God must go through a long night of rejection and solitude. Moses tended sheep on the backside of the desert, John the Baptist was born near Jerusalem but reached his greatness out in the desert, Jesus was tempted in the wilderness, and Paul withdrew for eight years in Arabia and Tarsus. Yet, have any others changed the world more than these?

The Don Stamps who emerged after his desert ordeal was a far different man than the one who first went to Brazil. Now he was more focused, more intense, and more humble. The years of preparation over; it was time to do his life's work.

GETTING STARTED AGAIN

There was absolutely no chance that Don and Linda and their three children could return to Brazil as missionaries under the banner of the Church of the Nazarene. They knew that if it was God's will for them to return to Brazil, they must find another church organization to send them.

Don knew he could not seriously go with any church unless he could agree with all its doctrines and practices. The truth was that he had been doing extensive study on speaking in tongues and knew his Pentecostal experience and theology would prevent him from joining any non-Pentecostal group.

In the summer of 1978, Linda was baptized in the Holy Spirit and spoke in other tongues. She had been seeking the infilling of the Holy Spirit for a long time, and the experience came while she was in prayer at the farm house. As she spoke in tongues, she felt warm from the top of her head to the soles of her feet.

It was a day of joy for Don and Linda Stamps. He decided to do what God had told him—"Go talk to that Assemblies of God preacher in Kansas City."

Don called Wesley, who arranged a meeting with U.S. Grant at a restaurant in Kansas City. Wesley asked Pastor Grant if he remembered the two Nazarene seminary students who had received the baptism in the Holy Spirit in his office years before. Pastor Grant only vaguely remembered the incident but immediately offered to help Don join the Assemblies of God.

The next day Don drove his old, third-owner Lincoln Continental with 130,000 miles on it across the state to Kansas City, Kansas, and Pastor Grant's office. He had many questions about the Assemblies of God. Don was now thirty-nine and knew that most church organizations did not like to bring on new missionaries past the age of thirty-five. Assemblies of God schools were graduating many missionary candidates. Where would he and Linda fit in? He asked Brother Grant, "Do you think the Assemblies of God will have me?"[1]

THE ASSEMBLIES OF GOD

The Assemblies of God had become one of the largest Protestant church bodies in the world and the largest foreign missions organization. The General Council of the Assemblies of God was formed at a meeting of 300

Pentecostal leaders in Hot Springs, Arkansas, in April, 1914. At that time a Pentecostal revival was sweeping many parts of America. The revival had its roots in the strong Holiness Movement that had resulted in many new church denominations, such as the Church of the Nazarene. The baptism in the Holy Spirit and speaking in tongues was the primary difference between the traditional holiness churches and the new "Pentecostal" churches.

Among the Pentecostals was widespread opposition to organizing officially into a denomination. However, many groups sought some sort of a fellowship that would promote cooperation among the different Pentecostal groups to increase publishing capabilities, help coordinate worldwide missionary evangelism, and promote ministerial education. The Hot Springs meeting was the result of a nationwide call for such cooperation.[2]

The Hot Springs General Council did not adopt a statement of faith but agreed that the Bible was "the all sufficient rule for faith and practice." Pentecostal publisher E.N. Bell was named the first general superintendent, although it was some years before that title was used. Two years later in 1916, the Assemblies of God General Council approved a "Statement of Fundamental Truths" that solidified the young group's beliefs and established its stance on the baptism in the Holy Ghost and speaking in tongues:

"All believers are entitled to and should ardently expect and earnestly seek the promise of the Father, the baptism in the Holy Ghost and fire....This was the normal experience of all in the early Christian Church. With it comes the enduement of power for life and service, the bestowment of the fruits and their uses in the work of the ministry (Luke 24:49; Acts 1:4, 8; I Cor. 12:1-31). This experience is

155

distinct from and subsequent to the experience of the new birth....With the baptism in the Holy Ghost come such experiences as an overflowing fullness of the Spirit..., a deepened reverence for God..., an intensified consecration to God and dedication to His work..., and a more active love for Christ, for His word, and for the lost....

"The baptism of believers in the Holy Ghost is witnessed by the initial physical sign of speaking with other tongues as the Spirit of God gives them utterance (Acts 2:4). The speaking in tongues in this instance is the same in essence as the gift of tongues (I Cor. 12:4-10, 28), but different in purpose and use."[3]

The Assemblies of God believed that sanctification was a progressive work rather than a distinct experience following salvation as the Nazarenes taught. Both the Assemblies of God and the Church of the Nazarene emphasized the need for living a holy life in the image of Christ.

Don began learning as much as he could about the Assemblies of God. He had studied its successful missions program in college and seminary; and now he wanted to know more about its theology. He liked what he found. The General Council, based in Springfield, Missouri, had recently expressed concern about liberal teaching in evangelical schools. Don's disgust for professors who doubted the inerrancy and full inspiration of the Bible was shared by the leaders of the Assemblies of God. He wholeheartedly agreed with the Assemblies of God stand for a separated and holy life; but the greatest attraction to the movement for Don was evangelism. The church emphasized the second coming of Christ and was committed to take the gospel to the whole world. Don wanted desperately to join the Fellowship and go back to Brazil as an Assemblies of God missionary.

He sent a cassette tape to Wesley, who had moved to Olathe, Kansas, to teach New Testament Studies at Mid-America Nazarene College. On the tape Don said:

"I want the zeal and passion that Paul had. He used tongues in his private devotions. I want to imitate him. Paul has always been my hero. Paul actually claimed to be a Pentecostal [1 Cor. 14:18]. If Paul was this, then you and I should be, too. I've been praying in tongues, and it really helps. Don't tell anyone at that Nazarene College or I'll tell on you. (Ha ha!)"[4]

THE ROAD TO ACCEPTANCE

U.S. Grant suggested that he and Don meet in Wichita with the Kansas Assemblies of God District Presbytery. That board was made up of District Superintendent Paul Lowenberg, Assistant District Superintendent U.S. Grant, District Secretary-Treasurer Derald Musgrove, and the presbyters of the sections into which the district was divided.

Paul Lowenberg had become one of the best-known Pentecostal preachers in America and served for many years as a member of the Executive Presbytery that governs the General Council of the Assemblies of God. Derald Musgrove later served for fourteen years as district superintendent in Kansas until his retirement in 1992.

The meeting was scheduled for February 15, 1978, at the Ramada Inn in Wichita. Don drove most of the night in a blizzard to visit his parents in Oklahoma City before going to Wichita. His stomach was tied in knots as he thought about the meeting with the Assemblies of God officials. He had no idea how they would react to him. He was a stranger and a Nazarene. Why would the Assemblies of God want him at age thirty-nine? To make matters worse, Don listened to

157

an eighteen-year-old evangelist on Jerry Falwell's radio program, "The Old Time Gospel Hour." A wave of depression and anxiety came over him like never before. He said of that experience:

"It was either a fleshly human depression or a satanic one, or both. It really hit me that here is an eighteen-year-old boy who is not wasting his life. I am twice his age and I haven't done anything for God yet. I felt hopeless and that I had blown the chance I had to serve God. Wasn't Paul forty-two before he began his ministry? That helps a little. I wish this thing hadn't hit me. I'm not sure how to handle it. I have asked the Lord to lift the depression, but he hasn't yet. Here I am running around like a nut wondering what I'm going to do. I stood for God's Word and lost everything, even my sanity was almost lost. The feeling I have is that God has given up on me. Sure, he might let me do a little, but it is too late to do something big for God. I just wish I hadn't listened to that program."[5]

Don felt like turning around and going back to the farm. Satan planted every conceivable negative thought in his mind about his failures and problems to try to convince him that he had no potential to become an Assemblies of God missionary.

There were more problems when Don arrived in Oklahoma City. He spent several hours with his younger brother Bobby who had stopped going to church and was involved in drugs. Don tried to talk to Bobby over lunch at a Chinese restaurant; but Bobby could not stand Don's aggressive attempts to talk some sense into him and got up and walked out of the restaurant during the meal. (Bobby, now called Bob, later rededicated his life to Christ during a glorious spiritual experience and is an active leader in his local church.)[6]

The next day Don drove to Wichita for the meeting. God had completely lifted his depression and replaced it with a fresh burden for the people of Brazil. His passion for and knowledge of the missionary effort in Brazil impressed the Assemblies of God officials. Paul Lowenberg remembers the meeting:

"I was impressed with Don's frankness, his clarity of thought, and I questioned him about his baptism. It was so real, so clear, so transforming that I said, 'Hey, this guy is for real!' He captured me in five minutes. He was so open and confessed his problems, his weaknesses. He was hanging up a mirror and telling us to look at him. That impressed me."[7]

Derald Musgrove had questions before the meeting. What was a man who was an expert in Greek doing on a farm in western Kansas? The meeting with Don totally changed his mind:

"He told us of his difficulty in Brazil. His straightforwardness, the appearance of integrity and honesty, and a genuine frustration as to how to get involved in the ministry in Brazil was obvious."[8]

Dr. Lowenberg suggested that U.S. Grant take Don to the Assemblies of God Headquarters in Springfield, Missouri, to talk to Loren Triplett, the Assemblies of God field secretary for Latin America. The meeting was set up for the next week. Brother Grant later explained his purpose in introducing Don to Loren Triplett:

"If I ever believed there was a man called by God, it was Don. He never lost his fervor to be a missionary to Brazil and its people. I really didn't know Don well, but God assured me that my one-hundred percent effort was necessary to get Don into the Assemblies of God...quickly."[9]

"Quickly" was the key word. Loren Triplett was immediately impressed with Don and told him of the pressing need for someone to help train the 50,000 Assemblies of God ministers and lay leaders in Brazil who were asking for help. The Assemblies of God missions effort in Brazil was exploding. Thousands of people were being saved each week, and dozens of new churches springing up. The need was great, and Don seemed perfectly fitted to fill an immediate place in the missions picture in Brazil. The field secretary told him it normally took two years for a new missionary to itinerate among local churches to raise the budget necessary to stay on the field.

Don said he couldn't wait that long.

The meeting ended with Don promising to go home to Goodland, talk with Linda, and seek God's will. Don and Linda fasted and prayed, and God spoke to them, saying, "You have fought for the Assemblies of God cause for so long! Why don't you join them?"[10]

The decision came quickly. On April 3, Don submitted his resignation as a Nazarene minister in a letter to Nazarene General Secretary B. Edgar Johnson:

"Over the past seven years I have been increasingly aware of the fact that the Church of the Nazarene and I are at variance on a most important tenet of the Christian faith, namely the inerrancy of the Word of God. It has always been my belief that the Bible in all that it contains has been inerrantly inspired by God. It now seems that the Church of the Nazarene has finally clarified the fact that it does not believe this....

"I feel that it would be better for the Church of the Nazarene and myself if I would join a church that affirms the total inerrancy of the Scriptures. It is a decision very difficult to make. Most of my friends are in the Church of the Nazarene. However, I cannot support an institution that has pledged itself to teach its men and women in its schools that they need only believe the Bible is partially inspired....

"I appreciate the Church of the Nazarene for the many things it has given me in the past. There are many brethren in the church—pastors, laymen, and professors—whom I dearly love. However, realizing that I am not a Nazarene with regard to my view of inspiration and that I do not want my three children to be taught they should not believe in the Bible in its entirety, I am leaving the Church of the Nazarene and am submitting my credentials."[11]

Don called Loren Triplett to tell him of his decision, and Triplett immediately asked Paul Lowenberg and the Kansas District Council to credential Don as an Assemblies of God minister and approve him and Linda as missionary candidates. The approval process occurred in record time; and in a matter of weeks a meeting was called to approve Don for ordination. Dr. Lowenberg enthusiastically supported the call for immediate action:

"I knew we couldn't do much for this fellow...but what he could do for us! I was in Brazil in 1971 and saw the possibilities. I was in a church with 41,000 members. It was fantastic! When Don came and spoke so knowledgeably of Brazil, I knew he was real because I had seen it for myself in Brazil."[12]

In just fourteen weeks from the date of his application, Don was ordained an Assemblies of God minister. God had done in four months what Don had tried to do for years.

161

TRAGEDY STRUCK!

Don and Linda began to wrap up the affairs on the farm and to attend an Assemblies of God church in nearby St. Francis, Kansas. There were still promises to be fulfilled to harvest wheat for other farmers.

In July, they were cutting Bob Silkman's wheat. Toby and Todd were spending a few days with Don's parents in Oklahoma City; and Tiffany was staying with a friend in town. Linda began her normal job of preparing the wheat truck for the trip into town to the grain elevators. She was tying a tarp over the load of wheat; and when she hopped down off the truck, her wedding ring caught on a nail and pulled the flesh completely off the bone of the ring finger!

At about the same time, Don drove up with the combine that needed refueling. He saw Linda's ring and finger laying on the ground.

Linda was in shock, and it was 50 miles to the nearest hospital!

Don wrapped Linda's hand in rags and picked up the finger and placed it in an ice chest. They jumped in their pickup truck and found Bob Silkman in the fields. Bob followed Don and Linda to the hospital in Goodland.

The doctor in Goodland saw how badly the finger was mangled and decided she should go by ambulance to Denver, 200 miles away. Linda's friend, Janet Moffett, got into the ambulance with Linda for the four-hour trek. However, the ambulance developed engine problems less than three miles from Goodland and had to turn back.

The Goodland hospital officials unsuccessfully tried to summon a helicopter to transport Linda to Denver. Not by coincidence, a specialist from Denver was working at the hospital that day and offered to fly Linda in his private plane to Denver.

She arrived at the Denver hospital six hours after the accident. The doctor did a beautiful job in removing the damaged finger and reconstructing the hand with three fingers and a thumb so that it is hardly noticeable.

Linda's parents went to Denver and took her home to Goodland. She worked hard in physical therapy and wondered how she could ever type again—or, more importantly, play the organ with a finger missing. She turned the problem over to God. Miraculously, Linda recovered dexterous use of her hand and played the organ and typed as skillfully as she had before the accident.[13]

MISSIONARY SUPPORT

Ron Iwasko, personnel secretary for the Assemblies of God Division of Foreign Missions, visited Don and Linda in Goodland to prepare the necessary applications for appointment to the mission field. In November, they traveled to Springfield to meet the Foreign Missions Administrative Committee to seek formal approval. Three weeks later they received the approval of the Foreign Missions Board, along with missionary candidates Gary and Wilma Davidson. Gary and Wilma [author Bob Burke's cousin] had grown up in the hills of southeast Oklahoma. They had met the Foreign Missions Administrative Committee because of their call from a successful pastorate in Haworth, Oklahoma, to the mission field in Ireland. God has blessed their work in Ireland, and they currently pastor one of the largest Protestant churches in that country.

The Division of Foreign Missions mandated that Don and Linda itinerate (travel from place to place) in local churches to raise an annual budget of about $25,000. As with all Assemblies of God foreign missionaries, the budget had to be secured before they would be allowed to go to the field. This practice has a threefold purpose: (1) It puts the responsibility of raising prayer and financial support on the missionaries; (2) It develops the missionaries from local pastors to ministers with a broader regional or national perspective; and (3) It exposes the local churches to the heart of world evangelism and missions.

The Stamps family moved to Wichita, Kansas, in December, 1978, and began itinerating among the churches to raise their support. Evangel Assembly of God in Wichita provided a church home and a house for the family to live in during that time.

Since Kansas had a relatively low population and small number of Assemblies of God churches, Derald Musgrove thought Don should seek support from his native state of Oklahoma. He and Jack Wilson took Don to Oklahoma City to meet District Superintendent Robert Goggin and the Oklahoma District Presbytery. Don explained his call to Brazil and told the Oklahoma leaders that if they ever backed off believing in the baptism in the Holy Spirit, speaking in tongues, or the inerrancy of the Bible, the church would not have to leave him but he would leave the church. The district officials could have seen Don's statement as arrogance; but instead the presbyters began clapping their hands, got excited, and all booked Don for a service before the afternoon was over. Don transferred his Assemblies of God credentials to Oklahoma and moved the family to Oklahoma City in August, 1979.

Don and Gary Davidson would touch base each Monday to see how each other had done in the weekend missionary services. Gary recalls:

"Don would go into little churches in western Oklahoma, tell his story of how he left the mission field and tried to make a living raising wheat and farming and how God never let him succeed. These old farmers would come up to him after the service, reach into their overalls, pull out of a wad of money, and hand it to him."[14]

During their missionary itineration, Don and Linda met fellow missionary candidates Quinton and Liz McGhee. Don and Quinton spent a lot of time hunting and fishing and camping out. Around the campfire after dark, the two would often get involved in deep theological discussions. Don shared with Quinton his call to Brazil. Quinton recalls his times with Don:

"Don was different from anyone I had ever met. He was like a prophet dropped down into a different century. He questioned everything most of us had come to accept. No single man has ever affected my life like Don Stamps did. Don asked me one day how much time I prayed each day. I told him it was none of his business. He relentlessly pursued the question until I promised to pray one hour a day. That commitment has changed my life. My ministry has flowed out of that hour a day in prayer.

"I loved Don very much. Our personalities were so different. He would talk so loudly in restaurants sometimes that I was embarrassed. But, even with his faults, Don was the greatest man of God and greatest missionary I have ever known in my life."[15]

Quinton and Liz McGhee have faithfully served as missionaries to Kenya since 1979.

Within a few months, Don's fund raising was so successful that he was fifty percent over his prescribed budget. District Superintendent Goggin called him in and asked him to curtail his itineration because other missionaries were trying to raise their budgets. Don then used some of his surplus pledges to help other missionaries who were struggling.

The events of the next thirteen years would make clear why it was important for Don to be the only Oklahoma missionary in anyone's memory to go to the field "over budget" and thus not have to return home occasionally to raise more funds.[16]

PRAYER MOUNTAIN

There was one matter of unfinished business. Don's parents had drifted away from God and the church. His mother had been saved at age twelve in a Presbyterian church and was active in the church youth group as a teenager. After she married Woody, church attendance was sporadic. They joined the Putnam City Methodist Church, but Satan provided many excuses to miss church services. Woody and Emma were never "fully committed to God."[17] Don felt strongly that he should not return to Brazil without sharing the gospel with his mother and father. In April, 1980, Don felt impressed to travel to South Korea to a place called Prayer Mountain to fast and pray for his parents' salvation.

Prayer Mountain is a prayer retreat established by Dr. Yonggi Cho, pastor of the world's largest church in Seoul, Korea, and his mother-in-law Jashil Choi. Cho had graduated in 1958 from a small Assemblies of God Bible school and, with Jashil Choi, began a tent church on the outskirts of Seoul. Later, in cooperation with Missionary John Hurston, Dr. Cho had developed a plan to divide his growing church into cell groups, each led by a competent lay leader. Rapid growth began, and hundreds of thousands of Koreans became active members of Yoido Full Gospel Church and other Assemblies of God churches in Korea.[18]

God had provided the $800 needed for the trip to Korea a year before. After Don had preached in a small church in Kansas, a farmer came up to him and handed over a wad of bills. Don thought it was a wad of one dollar bills and stuck it in his pocket. When he cleaned out his pockets that night, he counted the money. It was exactly $800. Don later explained in Pastor Cho's magazine why he had to go to Korea:

"The itineration had gone well. God had blessed, and we had raised more than adequate funds for our first four years in Brazil. It should have been a time of rejoicing, for our ministry as missionaries was about to begin. But there was one thing that hindered full joy. I was about to leave the United States, enter a foreign country, and preach the gospel to win souls for Christ; but I also was leaving behind my father and mother who were not Christians. They did not know Christ.

"This was a great burden on my soul. I prayed continually asking God what I should do. I knew that some way the power of Satan in their lives had to be broken, but this would be difficult. They were sixty-five years old, already retired; and it is not easy to win people of that age."[19]

Don didn't know what to expect in Korea. He rode a bus for forty-five minutes from the city of Seoul to Prayer Mountain. He was assigned a small cavelike room carved in the hillside. Don could not even stand up in the room. He fasted and prayed for seven days; and then God gave him the specific words he must use to speak to his parents about

Christ. He felt victory was near. He knew the fortresses that had been placed against his parents were beginning to fall. He fasted and prayed another three days.

Don arrived back in Oklahoma City late Saturday night. The next evening he told Toby and Todd, now ten and eight years old, that they were going to help him win Grandmother and Granddad to Christ. Linda stayed at home with Tiffany and prayed for the mission. When they arrived at Woody and Emma's house, Don sent the boys to the bedroom to pray. Don sat down at the kitchen table with his mom and dad. He first apologized for all the trouble he had caused them in his younger years. Then he told them the simple story of Jesus' love and death for them. For forty minutes Woody, Emma, and Don cried and hugged. And, for the first time in his life, Don saw his parents bow their heads and accept Jesus Christ into their hearts. It was a great day in the Stamps' house.[20]

The desert experience was over. When Don and Linda Stamps left for Campinas on August 7, 1980, it had been nine years since they had left Brazil.

PUSH BACK THE
DARKNESS

∞ *Chapter 11* ∞

Back to Brazil

*I*n the memory of missionaries still active today, travel to a foreign mission field was by steamship. For months in advance the missionaries would pack their belongings, supplies, and even canned foods in steel drums to be shipped by sea. In the Assemblies of God that tradition lives on in the Boys and Girls Missionary Crusade—the Sunday school missions program that raises millions of dollars each year for overseas literature such as Sunday school quarterlies, hymn books, Bible school textbooks, and other Christian education materials. The "mascot" for the children's program is Buddy Barrel, a cartoon-type character who is a missionary barrel ready to supply the missionaries with what they need for their ministry.

When the missionaries finally boarded a steamship—usually cabin space on a freighter—they would travel for weeks or even months before arriving at a port city, from which they would have to make their way by car, train, river boat, or on foot to their destination. The advantage was that they could make their adjustment slowly and be so glad to see their new home that it seemed almost normal to them.

Today's missionaries don't ship as many supplies because many products and equipment are available on their mission fields. The world in general has become more Westernized, and today's missionaries are able to adapt to the culture and live more as the local people do than in the past. Furthermore, they get on a jet airliner in America and arrive on their mission field in a matter of hours.

AN OPEN DOOR IN BRAZIL

The Stamps family—Don, Linda, Toby, Todd, and Tiffany— joined a staff of ten other Assemblies of God missionary couples in Brazil. For Don and Linda it was a joyous new beginning, and the opportunities for ministry were almost overwhelming. For the children it was a great adventure.

The Assemblies of God movement was exploding in Brazil and was by far the largest non-Catholic denomination. One visitor to that country said that everywhere he went in Brazil he found Coca Cola, Singer Sewing Machines, Bayer Aspirin, and the Assemblies of God.

By 1980, there were 14,000 churches with almost five million members and adherents served by 15,000 Brazilian ministers. Soul-winning exceeded all expectations as giant Good News Crusades (Assemblies of God evangelistic campaigns, often in tents, auditoriums, or stadiums) were held by well-known missionaries such as Bernhard Johnson—often called "the Billy Graham of Brazil." As many as 50,000 people attended nightly services in Brazil's largest cities. Thousands were being saved at each service.

Assemblies of God leaders felt a great responsibility to provide further biblical education for the new Christians. Many enrolled in correspondence courses through International Correspondence Institute (ICI), an educational arm of the Assemblies of God. Eighteen Bible schools were training about 1,500 students who expressed interest in deeper Christian service or full-time ministry. But, there were 26,000 applications for advanced Bible training. Even though Bible school classes were held day and night, there was no possible way to adequately train the thousands of new ministers being called to the new churches being planted each week.[1]

ACCEPTANCE AT LAST!

The Brazilian Assemblies of God—both the missionaries and the national church—accepted Don Stamps and his family immediately. Don's enthusiasm for open worship of God and his beliefs on holiness and separation from the world agreed with Brazilian standards.

Sunday night was the major weekly service in Assemblies of God churches with crowds larger than on Sunday morning. The service was filled with excitement because of the life-altering decisions made and the miracles of healing and deliverance that occurred. Brazilian Christians spent Sunday afternoons inviting their neighbors to church or preaching on street corners and in parks. Invariably many visitors were present at the Sunday night service, which Don described:

"The typical service begins with a lot of fervent prayer. Everyone prays out loud with hands raised as the presence of God is invoked. A lively song service follows with bands furnishing the accompaniment. People in Brazil love horns, especially loud horns. And they love choirs. As the people listen, they often will lift their hands in worship, tears streaming down their faces. They are so touched by the message. The singing is followed by what the Brazilians call "words." Two or three people, guests, young people being developed into spiritual leaders by the pastor, or others with a strong testimony will be called on to share a five-to-seven-minute "word." Those bringing the word will give it everything they

173

have for the few minutes allowed...very loud and very fervent.

"The preacher's message is always evangelistic. An often long altar call is a strong summary of what the preacher preached and exhorts the lost to seek Christ to save them, heal them, or deliver them. The pastors always conduct the altar call the same way by asking, 'Who will be first, who will be second, who will be third?' and so on. The rest of the congregation often joins those who have gone to the altar. There is much crying: tears often flow until the altar area is wet from weeping. Miracles often occur in this rich presence of the Lord, the presence which fuels the Brazilians' energetic and ever-spreading faith."[2]

Because the first Pentecostal missionaries were from Sweden, the Brazilian Assemblies of God churches have followed many of the practices of the Swedish Pentecostals. All established churches "mother" new works in their area with the goal of the new work becoming a self-supporting church. The new assemblies continue their relationship with the "mother" church and look to its pastor for guidance. These groups of churches, called "ministries," often include hundreds of churches with tens of thousands of believers.[3]

Don met head-on the challenge of providing Christian teaching for pastors and laymen alike. He felt his strong educational and seminary background equipped him well to teach Brazilians specific Pentecostal doctrines. Don wrote Wesley Adams back in the U.S.:

"The Assemblies of God lets me preach straightforward. I am being given the opportunity to help mold and create and form an educational system in Brazil. What a great influence I can have in that capacity. I can do this for 25 years.

Keep liberalism out and all other dangers in the educational system out! I have always been concerned about this type of thing, so this is a great miracle for me. God would want a person with a biblical basis, who believed in the absolute authority of the Word, an academically minded man, a man sensitive to the dangers that could come into an educational system, someone charismatic in the church. If this is valid, that fits me closely. So maybe in a unique way I will fit the Brazilian situation. I'm evangelistic enough to preach in their churches so it could be that a lot of my past history has prepared me in some way for all of this."[4]

Don and Linda reentered language school to learn Portuguese. Don also hired a tutor to help him ten to twenty extra hours per week. He wanted to speak Portuguese as well as the natives. He gave a progress report to Bob Silkman back in Goodland:

"It is not easy to learn a foreign language after the age of forty. I am speaking the language with hardly an accent, which is a miracle. I work at it three to four hours a day. Verbs are most difficult. They must have 60,000 verbs."[5] Don and Linda read the daily newspaper to help them with the language.

HOME AGAIN IN CAMPINAS

Family life in Brazil was wonderful for the Stamps. Don and Linda spent a lot of time making the transition from America to Brazil easier for the children. The family grew very close. Toby missed America the most because he was now eleven and very "Americanized." He had spent the first few years of school in Goodland, Wichita, and Oklahoma City, and began the fifth grade in Brazil. Todd was nine and was excited about returning to the country where he was born. He expected to see lions and tigers everywhere but had to settle for dogs, horses, donkeys, sheep, rabbits, turtles, and a milk cow Don bought to stock their *chacara*, or small acreage, outside Campinas. Tiffany was only three and never had any major problems adapting to the new Brazilian life.

The small farm, or chacara, was about eight miles out of Campinas on a hill overlooking a small Brazillian village. Looking back on those times, Linda said, "Don never left the farm, and the kids never did. We got that place because they wanted to live out in the country. Those years were probably the best years of our lives. We lived there for eight years. We had a lot of missionary activities out there. Not just the kids, but the parents liked to come out. We had a lot of beautiful flowering trees and shrubs, including one of those trees they call star fruit here in the States. When you cut it it looks like a star. Oh, I love those!"[6]

When asked about the children's schooling, Linda said, "They went into Campinas for school, but only for a half day. The Brazilians just go half a day because they have to use the school buildings for multiple classes. The younger children go in the mornings, the older kids in the afternoon, and the high school students at night."[7]

Linda spent most of her time taking care of the home and the children. Family was extremely important to Don. No matter how busy he was, he always took time when the kids came home from school to play with them and teach them Christian principles. Most evenings were spent around the fireplace with Don leading a family devotion and Linda reading a chapter from a book like *Robinson Crusoe*, *Penrod*, or *Kidnapped*. Don explained to the children the biblical standards of holiness and his desire that they would dedicate their lives to Christ. His love for Linda and the kids was unquestioned. As a disciplinarian, Don was tough. The two boys received regular spankings. All the missionary kids in Brazil informally voted Don as the father they would not want to spank them.

Don was still a farmer at heart, so the family hobby was raising and training horses. The three kids spent many hours with their father working with the horses and riding into the mountains.[8] Don reported on family life to his old farm friend, Bob Silkman:

"I am teaching the boys to be the best they can be. We are a family, a family that sticks together for Jesus, very fundamental in our beliefs, different from the world, and, frankly, different from much of the church. When the boys leave, it will take more than Satan and the world to break that loyalty to our family and our beliefs. We won't give in to sin and just any teaching that blows by. We are the Stamps family, and we don't suck eggs for anybody but Jesus."[9]

Toby and Todd were enrolled at the American School of Campinas, a secular school established for children of English-speaking foreigners (and a major reason why so many American missionaries continue to live there). Don became alarmed when a science teacher taught the theory of evolution. After one semester, the Stamps boys moved to the United Christian School, created for missionary children from all denominations. Don served as president of the school for two years. It was a small school with the highest enrollment at only twenty-five, but missionary parents helped the small staff teach the students in the Accelerated Christian Education (ACE) program, which allowed students to work at their own pace.[10]

TELEVISION

One of the few negatives for family life in Brazil was television. Don explained to Bob Silkman why the Stamps family did not have a television set:

"I feel that it is God's will. TV down here is much more immoral than in the States. It's nothing to see complete nudity of both men and women. The soap operas are awful. I decided not to allow my children to be raised up on a diet of Brazilian TV. Also, the majority of the Assemblies of God churches down here do not believe in TV and preach against it. To own a TV would weaken my ministry. I want as much influence with the pastors down here as I can have."[11]

Don's stand against television won him tremendous admiration from Brazilian Assemblies of God pastors. He developed an anti-television seminar for presentation around the country. (The full text of Donald Stamps' seminar notes appears in Appendix C of this book.)

Don could not believe how well the anti-television message was accepted:

"God is working hard on this TV thing. I am going every weekend to speak to another church. I am appearing at a church of 7,000 members this weekend. I have spoken to over 100,000 people this year about the evils of television. I have an eight-point study on television. It emphasizes my belief that TV destroys the work of the Holy Spirit in our lives, it destroys the grace of God in us, desensitizes us to sin, and changes our values and our actions."

Don took the anti-television message to all parts of Brazil, 2,000 miles to the north and 1,000 miles to the south. By air, by car, and by jeep he preached the message with the help of a projector and a printed pamphlet. He preached to as many as 9,000 people in one service and taught up to 1,500 ministers at each session. One night 5,500 people packed a church while another 1,500 listened to the message on loudspeakers outside. He received so many invitations that he was booked up for nine months in advance. Even the Baptist Publishing House in Brazil asked for permission to use Don's manual on television.

The impact of Donald Stamps' crusade against television was evident in all parts of Brazil. About 200 miles into the mountains was a town that had never had access to television until 1982. The local Assemblies of God church had 4,000 members, and none had been exposed to the ungodly programs on Brazilian television. The local pastor was terrified when the town installed a booster antenna and many of his members bought a television. His daughter was very sick. He had a vision one night in which God told him He was sad and hurt over the sickness of the daughter and sad and hurt over the church accepting television. In the vision several Portuguese words were written in the sky. He could not read them but could not forget them. The pastor attended a state convention of churches where Don was putting on his seminar. The letters he had seen in the sky in the vision were the same blue-lettered Portuguese words that Don projected on the wall of the auditorium to begin his seminar. The pastor knew immediately God was talking to him about preaching against television. He bought a hundred of Don's seminar notebooks and took them back into the mountains. He preached three nights from the notebook. A revival broke out, everyone who had bought a television sold it the next week, and hundreds of new converts were won to Christ.[12]

SPIRITUAL WARFARE

Spiritism (often called spiritualism, a religious belief system that centers on the influence of spirits and often deals with the spirits of the dead) is a major enemy of the church in Brazil. By 1986 there were 30 million spiritists who believed that men and women could contact spirits and influence them to act and intervene in situations according to the desires of the spiritist. The practice is so widespread in Brazil that pictures of the spiritist saints appear on postage stamps. Professional sports teams and even politicians contact spiritists for guidance.

Loren O. Triplett, then Assemblies of God Latin American field director and now foreign missions executive director, sent word that missionaries needed to understand fully that spiritual warfare was occurring in Brazil with the explosion of Pentecost. Don and the other Assemblies of God missionaries placed a strong emphasis on God and His supernatural power, including the casting out of demons, in the fight against spiritism.[13]

BIBLE NOTES FOR BRAZILIANS

Don was concerned for the thousands of pastors in Brazil who had no Bible school training and few, if any, books to help prepare for preaching. His concern was shared by fellow Assemblies of God missionaries David and Sherry Harrison who had been on the field since 1970. Don and Linda met the Harrisons during their Nazarene days in Brazil; and Don even had shared with David his secret of having the baptism in the Holy Spirit. When the Harrisons returned to Brazil in 1982 from itineration in the U.S., the two families became very close.

As Don began to write notes on the New Testament for the Brazilian pastors, David, or "Harry" as Don called him, recalled a typical Don Stamps night:

"Don had an exceptional mind. He was always a hundred miles ahead of you. My day started at 5 a.m., and I tried to get to bed by 9 or 10 at night. Invariably, Don would call about bedtime and say, 'Harry, we're going for a walk.' I would say, 'No I can't. I just got to bed.' Don would say, 'What a fine friend you are. I've been working on this book all day, it's all in my head, I've got to clear it out, or I'll never sleep.'

"We lived about ten miles away, so Don would come over or we would meet halfway and go for a long walk. He talked about the Scriptures he had been writing about that day. We would ask each other questions. If something puzzled him, he would go home and spend all night with his Bible and his precious books trying to find the answer."[14]

It may come as a surprise to today's readers of Donald Stamps' notes in the Zondervan Publishing House copies of *The Full Life Study Bible* in the New International Version or the King James Version that his favorite English Bible translation was the New American Standard Bible. According to Linda, that was the one he always had open on his work table. With his knowledge of ancient Greek, he felt that the NASB was the most literal and accurate of the modern translations.

THE BRAZILIAN FAMILY

In 1984 tragedy struck the Harrison family. Their seventeen-year-old daughter Denette, nicknamed Dee Dee, was killed in a motorcycle accident on the way to a pizza party to celebrate her being named valedictorian of her graduating class. Dee Dee was only three months away from graduation. She was a gifted student with a photographic memory and scored so well on the SAT test that several American universities had recruited her.

Don and Linda helped the Harrisons weather the storm. In their walks at night Don quoted Scriptures to help David realize that Dee Dee was better off in the presence of the Lord.[15]

The Assemblies of God missionaries in Brazil were a large "family." The Stamps fellowshipped with Randall and Claudia Walker, Carl and Terri Gibbs, Mark and Helba Lemos, Bruce and Karen Braithwaite, Gary and Jeanne Royer, Bob and Bev Combs, Jim and JoAnn Burton, John and Dorris Lemos, Bernhard and Doris Johnson, Eldon and Twyla Tracy, Dave and Sherry Harrison, and Rick and Sharon Hoover. Rick Hoover spent nine years of his childhood in Brazil with his missionary parents, Reg and Mary Hoover. At age eighteen he returned to the U.S. to attend Central Bible College in Springfield, Missouri. He and his wife Sharon began their missionary service in Brazil in 1978. Rick recalls the first time he met Don at the annual Missionary Fellowship in October, 1980:

"I believe Don and I 'clicked.' He was a very, very good friend and brother. I look back on our times together and remember wonderful, crazy, reaching-for-righteousness, contending-for-truth moments. Don was a very intense person. His thirst for truth was insatiable. He was a thinker, prober of deep matters. He enjoyed his family very much. He believed powerfully in raising his children in the nurture and admonition of the Lord.

"He was a man of strong convictions. And he let you know where he stood regarding the big issues. He would get very upset with sin and degradation in the world."[16]

SECRETS OF THE BRAZILIAN PENTECOSTAL REVIVAL

Don felt the Assemblies of God in Brazil was a modern example of what the gospel of Christ can accomplish when preached with full conviction and in the power of the Holy Spirit. By the time Don and Linda left Brazil in 1988 to work full-time on *The Full Life Study Bible*, there were nine million Assemblies of God members and adherents and 21,000 churches in Brazil. Don cited four basic reasons for the miraculous growth:

"First, *Pentecostal truth*. They are constantly preaching the Pentecostal message to anyone and everyone who will listen. They are not ashamed to preach the Word in any town or to any neighbor or stranger. Christ has changed their lives.

"Second, *The power of the Holy Spirit*. Their lives and proclamation of the Pentecostal gospel are done in the power of the Holy Spirit. They seek and rely on the Holy Spirit to bring conviction of sin, save the lost, heal their afflictions, and help them in their daily lives. I personally have witnessed a single service where hundreds were baptized in the Spirit. That particular service lasted four hours and was marked by extraordinary spiritual hunger, intense seeking of God, hundreds prostrate in prayer, and tears to such an extent that you could not walk on dry ground at the altar area.

"Third, *Great conviction*. They have no doubts about the Word of God. Reality for them is in the sphere of Christ and communion with the Holy Spirit, and spiritual things are seen as a matter of life and death.

"Fourth, *Separation from the world*. They are a separated people and endeavor to live a holy and blameless life before God. When one is converted and becomes an Assemblies of God believer, he is taught immediately that he must reject his old lifestyle of sinful habits and worldly pleasures. He is to turn from sin and become one with a community of believers seeking to live for God and wait for Christ to return to His church."[17]

PUSH BACK THE
DARKNESS

∽ *Chapter 12* ∾

It Began with a Few Notes

*D*on felt that he had wasted many years of his life before he got to accomplish His calling. And yet, the tragedies and sufferings of those difficult years produced the man who could accomplish the extraordinary task of putting a new study Bible in the hands of Pentecostal and Charismatic people around the world.

A VISION FOR A PENTECOSTAL STUDY BIBLE

The inspired vision for a Pentecostal study Bible was birthed in Don before he ever returned to Brazil in 1980. He was aware that thousands of new Pentecostal pastors and leaders in new churches had no Bible school training and no Pentecostal study notes to help them teach new converts.

While still raising his missionary support, Don called fellow missionary candidate Gary Davidson and asked, "What Bible has been the most popular in evangelical Christianity?" When Gary didn't have an immediate answer, Don said God had asked him the same question. The obvious answer was the Scofield Reference Bible, which had been the most popular study Bible for all evangelicals since its release in 1909. Don had told Wesley Adams that his problem with the Scofield Bible was its major doctrinal differences with Pentecostals on vital issues such as eternal security, gifts of the spirit, and the baptism in the Holy Spirit. He and Wesley spent hours dreaming out loud about their collaboration on a comprehensive study Bible.[1]

Don's vision for a study Bible was very similar to that of C.I. Scofield a century earlier. Both were missionaries. Both saw the need to teach doctrine to new converts so that a solid foundation of faith would remain after the emotion of the initial salvation experience. Scofield was a successful lawyer when he was converted to Christ by a client who boldly witnessed to him in St. Louis in 1879. He pastored in Dallas and became a renowned Bible scholar before God gave him a burden for the lost in Central America. It was during missionary trips to Costa Rica that God placed in Scofield's heart the need for a study Bible.[2]

The only other study Bible written from a Pentecostal viewpoint had met only limited success. Assemblies of God theologian Finis Jennings Dake had published a Bible in 1961. It was extremely well-researched, but Pentecostal leaders and theologians never fully endorsed the Dake Bible because it was frequently given to speculation, took passages out of context, and advanced novel theories such as a pre-Adamite world.[3]

Don had another reason for wanting a Pentecostal study Bible. He was greatly concerned about the way many Pentecostal churches were changing in America. He felt Pentecostals were compromising many of their original convictions, such as being a separated people living holy lives before God. He feared the explosion of television evangelism was resulting in what he called "surface salvation," where people were supposedly getting saved but never becoming true disciples of Jesus Christ. Don felt strongly that the local church was the key to discipling new Christians where the "pastor lived with a people, laughed with them, cried with them, saw their babies born, and preached the pure Word of God."[4] Don felt a local pastor could feed his congregation much better if he had a study Bible to help in preparation of sermons.

THE VISION UNVEILED

Don unveiled his vision in a March 17, 1980, letter to Loren O. Triplett:

"Friday I spoke in chapel at CBC [Central Bible College in Springfield, Missouri]. Many of the students either had a Scofield or a Ryrie Study Bible. Both of them are highly Calvinistic and anti-Pentecostal. I firmly believe we need our own study Bible. Not that I am wanting to write or edit one for us here in the States. I am a missionary, so my burden is for our people in Brazil. However, this does point out that there is a need and desire for such a work.

"I would like to ask for permission to begin now to gather material and ideas for the Brazilian study Bible. During my first four years in Brazil I could continue to build data, collect materials, and develop ideas. I need to learn what our Brazilian people and pastors need and to learn where they are having trouble.

"I want the study Bible to be more than one with a few academic notes. I want it to move our people toward a right belief and right living, toward truth and righteousness. I believe that the Christian church is being attacked and many times penetrated by ungodly philosophies, secularism, liberalism, humanism, worldliness, and materialism."[5]

Don had five major goals for the Brazilian study Bible: (1) A commentary on major doctrines from a Pentecostal perspective; (2) an explanation of the Bible that a Christian could use for developing a deeper walk with Christ; (3) a tool to combat and expose false doctrines such as predestination, liberalism, spiritism, and ideas of men; (4) a present-day look at problems of marriage, divorce, pornography, and homosexuality; and, (5) a straightforward presentation of biblical principles regarding subjects such as prayer, fasting, and money.[6]

Don asked permission to use $2,000 of the funds he had raised for his missionary budget to pay for the preliminary work on the study Bible. He needed additional books for his library and a computer to begin the massive job of researching, writing, typing, and arranging the study notes. The Foreign Missions Administrative Committee, led by Executive Director J. Phillip Hogan, gave its endorsement of the project and approved the initial expenditure.

THE PROJECT BEGINS

Don began his work on the study Bible shortly after he and Linda arrived back in Brazil. He taught in the Bible school in the city of Pindamonhangaba and wrote material for the Brazil Extension School of Theology (BEST) in Campinas—a three-hour drive apart. When he was not traveling to give his anti-television seminar or preaching in outlying areas he was reading and researching in his large theological library and writing notes for Linda to type and arrange in the computer.

His burden for the national pastors was heavy. He was asked to write a correspondence course on 1 and 2 Corinthians to be used by BEST,[7] and within a few months the course was ready and distributed in Portuguese throughout Brazil.

Don and Linda knew their direction was changing. The momentous task of writing study notes on the entire Bible would consume their lives for almost a decade.

A PROJECT FOR THE WORLD

Until 1983 the scope of the study Bible project was still limited to a Brazilian edition in Portuguese. Don wrote Bob Silkman in Goodland:

"We have started on the study Bible. It will take four or five days a week to work on it. Once we really get into it, it will be hard to quit and do other missionary assignments. I've already written the Book of Acts, and I'm going to start with Matthew in the next couple of days. I've got about 150 comments that I will want to use in Matthew. Some large, some small. It will take two or three months. Mark and Luke won't take as long since I made so many comments in Matthew. John will take a little longer. I am researching and teaching Romans already at 'Pinda.' I've already done a lot of research in writing the correspondence course on 1 and 2 Corinthians. I ought to have the New Testament knocked out in a year."[8]

The visionary Don Stamps was typically over-optimistic. The deeper he went into his comments on the New Testament, the more time the project demanded. He and Linda worked on through 1983 and 1984. It was customary for Assemblies of God missionaries to serve a four-year term and return to the U.S. for at least a year to renew their financial support while reporting to local churches about their missionary efforts. As usual, Don was different. He wrote:

"God has given me the strength and desire to stay here. I don't want to go home and waste precious time itinerating from church to church. They want to buy a new computer for Linda. They want to bring me back to the States twice a year to go over all the work."[9]

THE EDITORIAL COMMITTEE

By 1983, the Assemblies of God Division of Foreign Missions began to see the potential of the study Bible as a worldwide project for many languages. The Foreign Missions Administrative Committee committed $10,000 per month for two years to the project. Loren Triplett worked with Don to make a list of theologians to serve on the Editorial Committee to scrutinize Don's work. Triplett wanted to make certain that the study Bible accurately reflected doctrinal views of the Assemblies of God. Life Publishers International, the department of the Assemblies of God that distributes foreign language materials, became involved and endorsed the idea of an Editorial Committee. A prestigious group of men was brought together, consisting of Dr. J. Wesley Adams (associate editor), Dr. Stanley M. Horton (chairman), Dr. William W. Menzies (co-chairman), Dr. French Arrington, Robert Shank, Roger Stronstad, Dr. Richard Waters, and Bishop Roy L.H. Winbush.[10]

DR. J. WESLEY ADAMS, PH.D.

Don's first choice for someone to help on the Bible was his closest and dearest comrade, Wesley Adams; but Wesley was still a professor at Mid-America Nazarene College in Olathe, Kansas. Nazarene officials obviously did not know Wesley had received the baptism in the Holy Spirit. If Wesley assisted in the preparation of a Pentecostal study Bible, he would be forced to reveal his beliefs.

Wesley's life had changed for the better since Don and Linda had returned to Brazil. Fellow professor Larry Fine and other friends convinced him that he should reconsider his not getting married because of his handicap. When Jane Peterson, one of his former students who had graduated from college with highest honors, expressed interest in him in conversations with mutual friends, Wesley was stunned. They courted for a year and were married on May 9, 1981.

Wesley had been the leader of weekly prayer meetings at Mid-America Nazarene College since 1980. In the classroom he avoided his personal testimony about receiving the baptism in the Holy Spirit but did treat honestly all topics about the Holy Spirit in the Scriptures. This openness about the Holy Spirit made him a popular professor with the students but raised eyebrows among college administrators. The weekly prayer meetings in Wesley's home bore fruit; there were miracles, and students were growing in their hunger for the full range of the Holy Spirit's ministry.[11]

In the spring of 1983, the college administration asked Wesley to declare his view of speaking in tongues. He honestly told them what he believed the New Testament taught. He was told he could not hold that view and teach in a Nazarene college. He and three other professors—Ron Lawlor, Arlie Peck, and Mark Wilson—submitted their resignations to college president Curtis Smith after a debate over whether tongues was actually being taught in the classroom.

The local newspaper reported the story:

"The issue of speaking in tongues is one that has caused emotional divisions within the Nazarene church in the past.... None of the teachers resigning say they have taught, advocated, or promoted speaking in tongues in their classes. But at the core of the dispute is a Friday evening prayer session started a couple of years ago first on campus and then later switched to Wes Adams' house. Adams said that during some of his own private prayer sessions he has spoken in tongues. 'This is the first time I've let anyone know this publicly. Many of my students and friends will be surprised to hear it,' Adams said.

"Non-Nazarenes, or those who are not familiar with the charismatic movement, may find the whole tongues issue baffling. More understandable is what may be a deeper issue involving church authority. There is no statement in the Manual (that small black book which is the written record of the ruling body of the Nazarene denomination, the General Assemblies which meet every four years) outlawing speaking in tongues. There is no reference to speaking in tongues at all. Some Nazarenes maintain that since the issue is not directly addressed in the Manual, it is open to scriptural and theological quest.

"MANC (Mid-America Nazarene College) administration and its Board...maintain that an official statement in the church organ "Herald of Holiness" clarifies the tongues issue.... The Board has ruled that 'practice or propagation of speaking in tongues...shall be interpreted as inveighing against the doctrines and usages of the Church.'"[12]

In his resignation letter to Dr. Smith, Wesley said, "I have always expressed with candor my understanding of what the New Testament teaches on any subject. 'Tongues' has been no exception. My position on it is not a recent one, and I cannot change it now for the sake of my job. I choose to continue to submit to the supreme authority of God and His Word. In the words of Martin Luther, 'Here I stand. I can do no other.'"[13]

By August, 1983, Wesley, knowing that he could not stay in the Nazarene Church, submitted his ordination credentials to the general secretary at the Nazarene headquarters in Kansas City. The prayer meeting at Wesley's home resulted in the birth of Olathe Fellowship, which four years later joined Metro Vineyard Fellowship, a charismatic church that has grown to weekly attendance of several thousand. Wesley continues to serve as one of the church's pastors as well as a teacher at Grace Training Center of Kansas City.

With this turn of events, Wesley was now free to join Don and Linda's team to complete the study Bible. He began active work as associate editor in April, 1984, and began work as author alongside Don in 1987.

DR. STANLEY M. HORTON, TH.D.

Stanley M. Horton is a third-generation Pentecostal who has authored several theological books with an emphasis on the working of the Holy Spirit. He was introduced to Pentecost as a child. His grandmother received the baptism in the Holy Spirit in the late 1800's, and the heritage was passed down to Dr. Horton through his Methodist father who also received the experience and spoke in tongues. His degrees include a B.S. from the University of California, an M.Div. from Gordon-Conwell Theological Seminary, an S.T.M. from Harvard University, and a Th.D. from Central Baptist Theological Seminary. He wrote the adult teacher Sunday school quarterly for the Assemblies of God for a quarter century. He taught at Central Bible College for thirty years and was Distinguished Professor of Bible and Theology at the Assemblies of God Theological Seminary for thirteen years. Since 1990, Dr. Horton has been general editor of Logion Press, the academic book line of Gospel Publishing House.[14]

DR. WILLIAM W. MENZIES, PH.D.

Dr. William Menzies was named co-chairman of the Editorial Committee. He earned a B.A. at Central Bible College, a B.A. and M.A. at Wheaton College, and a Ph.D.

in American Church History at the University of Iowa. He was commissioned to write the official history of the Assemblies of God, entitled *Anointed to Serve* (Gospel Publishing House, 1971). Dr. Menzies has been a success- ful pastor and is recognized worldwide in missions educa- tion. After teaching at Central Bible College, Evangel College, and the Assemblies of God Theological Seminary and serving as a vice president of the California Theological Seminary, he now is the president of Asia Pacific Theological Seminary in Baguio City, Philippines.[15]

DR. FRENCH ARRINGTON, PH.D

Dr. French Arrington represented the Church of God (Cleveland, Tennessee) on the Editorial Committee. A scholar in every sense of the word, he received his B.A. at the University of Tennessee at Chattanooga, an M.Div. and Th.M. from the Colombia Theological Seminary and a Ph.D. at St. Louis University in Biblical Languages. He has lec- tured around the world and has taught at Southeastern Bible College and Lee College. He has been a professor of New Testament Greek and Exegesis at the Church of God School of Theology since 1975. He has authored a number of books.[16]

ROBERT SHANK, A.B., D.H.L.

Robert Shank came to the committee from a Baptist her- itage. His father was a successful Baptist pastor. After teach- ing for more than a decade in a Baptist academy established by his father, Rev. Shank broke with Baptist tradition and published two books—*Life in the Son* in 1960 and *Jesus: His Story* in 1962. Both books disagreed with the traditional Baptist teaching of eternal security and resulted in Shank

196

being asked to leave his Southern Baptist Church. Don Stamps and Jim Dimick had read Shank's books during their college days at BNC. Don was very impressed with Shank both as a scholar and a Christian leader.[17]

ROGER STRONSTAD, M.C.S.

Roger Stronstad is a professor at the Western Pentecostal Bible College, affiliated with the Pentecostal Assemblies of Canada. He is the author of a widely acclaimed book, *The Charismatic Theology of St. Luke.*

RICHARD WATERS, D.MIN.

Dr. Richard Waters is a longtime leader of the Pentecostal Holiness Church. He graduated with honors with a B.A. in religion from North Carolina Wesleyan College, received an M.Div. from Duke University and a D.Min. from Phillips University. He accepted Jesus as his Savior at age sixteen and pastored churches in Oklahoma and his native North Carolina before beginning a long career as a scholar and religious educator. He currently is academic dean at Holmes College of the Bible in Greenville, South Carolina.

Dr. Waters also served on the committee that produced the *Rainbow Study Bible.*[18]

BISHOP ROY L. H. WINBUSH, M.DIV., D.D.

Bishop Roy L.H. Winbush is a member of the General Board of the Church of God in Christ, one of the largest Pentecostal groups in the world. Bishop C.H. Mason organized the denomination in a tent in the early years of the twentieth century in Lexington, Mississippi. Bishop Winbush grew up in southern Louisiana but was on the other side of the planet when God called him to preach during the Korean War. He wanted to be a professor at Southern University where he had graduated before entering the U.S. Army. God spoke clearly to him about his call to the ministry. His first sermon, "God Wants a Man", was preached to three men in the hills of South Korea.

After graduation from the New Orleans Baptist Theological Seminary, he pastored churches and for many years served as the president of his denomination's publishing board. He was editor-in-chief for Sunday school material for the ten thousand Churches of God in Christ.[19]

COOPERATIVE EFFORTS

The Editorial Committee members were spread all over the globe from Canada to Missouri to the Philippines. With Don and Linda still living in Brazil, the work of the committee had to be accomplished through the mail. When Don completed notes, he sent them first to Wesley. Their long friendship had resulted in Don giving Wesley complete freedom to delete notes that he thought were unnecessary, to add notes, or to completely rewrite them. Don respected Wesley's judgment biblically, theologically, and literarily.

After Wesley edited the notes, he sent them to the committee members for their comments and revisions. The team worked well together, even though the members sometimes disagreed over an interpretation or about how to emphasize specific sections. The give and take was honest and sincere. For example, on one occasion, Roger Stronstad wrote Don:

"Your comments on Acts 13:2 in regard to social concerns...are highly questionable. The whole subject of baptism-filling for vocation as prophets needs to be emphasized far more than it is."[20]

198

Don accepted the revisions in the right spirit. He and the committee wanted the study Bible to be accurate and in the best form possible. Many subjects were bounced around among the members for weeks before a final draft was completed. Wesley took on the responsibility of writing the introduction to each of the sixty-six books of the Bible. Linda spent most of her waking hours typing the notes on the computer.

The committee members developed warm friendships and all shared Don's vision to create a strong study Bible from the Pentecostal and holiness perspective. Dr. Menzies looks back on the project:

"I was struck by the sacrifice Don was willing to make, laying aside an evangelistic ministry which was in demand, to devote himself with discipline to the isolation and tedium of scholarly work. That Don and Linda were able to work out a livable schedule for themselves that required years of painstaking work is itself a high commendation.... There are no similar precedents in Assemblies of God missions... Don had the strong support of his Latin American boss, Loren Triplett, but it was Don who had to shape the strategy and to pursue the enterprise. Don had an unswerving vision, and tireless commitment to achieving the goal he felt God had assigned to him.... He would call on frequent occasions, often from half-way around the world. He arranged for regular meetings with me, usually in Springfield, once in Brazil.... When we got together, we would go over each page. Sometimes we stopped and engaged in lengthy discussion over various points."[21]

Dr. Menzies and other committee members tried for a balance in Don's strong call for a life of separation and holiness. "I felt the need to be a 'gadfly,' to argue from the side of grace," Dr. Menzies wrote. Often Don modified his stance. Dr. Menzies saw Don grow during the project:

"I watched his growing maturity and his growing breadth of insight. He did not waver in his strong commitment to keep the values of the revival clear, but he did exhibit a growing charity of spirit and breadth of outlook."[22]

About 60 percent of the New Testament notes were written by 1987, but no publisher for the English language version had been selected. Life Publishers International was preparing to publish the New Testament in Portuguese, Spanish, and Korean; but another publisher was needed for the English version.

ZONDERVAN PUBLISHING HOUSE

In early 1988, Bob Hoskins, president of Life Publishers, was having lunch with Bruce Ryskamp, corporate vice president of Zondervan Publishing House in Grand Rapids, Michigan. When he mentioned the study Bible project in Brazil, Ryskamp was interested. He contacted Don Stamps and asked for a sample of the notes.

Zondervan had grown from two men working out of their garage to a major religious publishing company with hundreds of employees and many bookstores. Today it is a division of Harper Collins Publishers.

In January, 1989, Zondervan's theological editor Verlyn Verbrugge was assigned the task of reading Don's notes on the Gospels and Ephesians to evaluate whether the company should undertake the project. His first impression was that the publication of the Bible would not be economically sound because Zondervan had never published a study Bible involving one particular denomination. Also, initially, he was concerned with the dogmatic style of Don's writing. He was afraid he could not work with an author with such strong views. Yet he knew there was a large group of Pentecostals and Charismatics in the world who did not have their own study Bible. His comments were passed along to his superior, Doris Rikkers, the director of Publications. As a marketing decision, Zondervan's Product Planning Committee approved the project and invited Don to Grand Rapids.

At the first meeting, Verlyn Verbrugge changed his mind about Don. He found him to be completely open to suggestions and "someone we could work with."[23] Work on the notes got very serious after that meeting. Verbrugge was assigned as project editor. One of the early problems he saw with the notes was the length of comments on certain passages, but he decided to turn the lengthy notes into separate articles.

By the middle of 1988, the logistics of trying to complete the New Testament notes from Brazil were too difficult. Don and the Division of Foreign Missions decided that the Stamps should return to Springfield, Missouri, to live until the notes were completed. The family was filled with sadness as they left Brazil for a second time. They arrived in Springfield in December, 1988.

Zondervan developed an aggressive deadline for the project. Don and the Editorial Committee had until September 15, 1989, to finalize the New Testament notes, articles, and introductions. Verbrugge wanted to get to know Don better and used his vacation to travel to Springfield to be with him. Their weekend together resulted in a strong bond of friendship. Verbrugge is an ordained minister in the Christian Reformed Church and had authored the *NIV Topical Study Bible* a few years earlier. After pastoring churches for 16 years, he completed his doctorate at the University of Notre Dame in 1988 and joined Zondervan.

Verbrugge and his colleague Dirk Buursma had early problems with Don's articles on wine. Their position was that New Testament references to wine always meant fermented wine. The thoroughness of Don's historical and theological research convinced them their position was wrong.[24]

After eleven months of editing and proofreading, the New Testament was ready for national release in Bible bookstores in August, 1990. Zondervan decided to call the English version, *The Full Life Study Bible*, rather than the "Pentecostal Study Bible" as the foreign language editions were labeled. Zondervan felt that deleting the word "Pentecostal" would allow the Bible to be marketed more widely to Charismatics and other interested believers who were not Pentecostal but who could benefit from the study Bible.

AN ACCLAIMED SUCCESS

The finished New Testament was superb. The study notes provided extensive Scripture references to assist the reader in in-depth study of the Bible. Forty-two articles on important biblical topics were distributed throughout the text, articles on topics such as the doctrine of the Holy Spirit, the ministry gifts to the church, divine healing, parents and children, standards of sexual morality, the rapture, and personal apostasy. The Bible had a subject index, charts, maps and a concordance. On many pages of the Bible appeared symbols in the margin representing major themes such as "Filled With the Holy Spirit," "Gifts of the Holy Spirit," "Fruit of the Spirit," "Healing," "Faith," and "Witnessing." The "Themefinders" system allowed the reader to study one of the six topics and find in the margin the reference to the next text on that particular theme. The introduction to each Bible book included an outline of the book, an explanation of its background and original purpose, a survey, a list of the book's special features, and was expanded to include a suggested reading plan that would enable the reader to cover the New Testament within one year.

National and international leaders praised the new study Bible. David Wilkerson, author of *The Cross and the Switchblade*, and pastor of the Times Square Church in New York said, "*The Full Life Study Bible* comes at just the right time to strengthen the roots of evangelical Christianity. It is needed to promote holiness and scriptural understanding."[25]

Leonard Ravenhill, a renowned evangelical author with numerous books on revival, said he wished he would have had this Bible when he was a young man: "It would have directed me to God's principles concerning holiness and life in the Holy Spirit. Its emphases are of vital importance for the church in this hour of history."[26]

Pastor Yonggi Cho of the Yoido Full Gospel Church in Seoul, Korea, wrote, "This Bible repeatedly emphasizes the absolute priority of New Testament truth, devotion to Christ, a righteous life, and the manifested power of the Holy Spirit."[27]

The last paragraph of Don's "Author's Preface" to the New Testament of *The Full Life Study Bible* summed up his feelings:

"Throughout these years of labor I have felt a profound sense of weakness and unworthiness to expound on God's holy Word. Many times I have been driven to my knees in need of special grace and help. I can testify that God, who is rich in mercy and whose grace is sufficient, has sustained me by his Spirit. Through all the long days and hours his Word has spoken to my heart. My desire for a full manifestation of Biblical Christianity has deepened and developed into an intense longing that is surpassed only by my longing for that day of the appearing of our Lord and Savior. With thanks to God—the Father, the Son and the Holy Spirit— for the privilege of laboring in the Scriptures, I send forth this work unto him who loves us and gave himself for us so that we may have life and have it to the full."[28]

A WORLDWIDE PROJECT

Don and the Editorial Committee had completed about half of *The Full Life Study Bible* notes on the Old Testament by the time the New Testament was published. They were working toward a September, 1991, deadline for submission of the Old Testament notes. The Assemblies of God Division of Foreign Missions, now under the leadership of Loren Triplett, continued to make *The Full Life Study Bible* a major project. Executive Director Loren Triplett served as chairman of a special Bible Committee to make final editorial decisions. Other members of the committee were Don, Wesley Adams, William Menzies, Stanley Horton, and Bob Hoskins.

Brother Triplett was especially interested in the Bible notes being translated into the major languages of the world. He had served as a missionary to Nicaragua for 13 years before becoming head of Life Publishers. During his term as a missionary, his years at Life Publishers, and as the Assemblies of God field secretary for Latin America, he had prayed for the opportunity to provide a Pentecostal study guide for national ministers and congregations around the world. The project vision that Don had brought to his desk a decade before was alive and well.[29]

It was decided to call the foreign language translations "The International Pentecostal Study Bible." In September, 1990, Joseph W. Kilpatrick, executive vice president of Life Publishers, was appointed as International Project Coordinator to lead the effort to translate Don's notes into some 25 major languages of the world. Kilpatrick had been associated with the Division of Foreign Missions since 1966. He had served as finance director for DFM, as a missionary with International Correspondence Institute in Belgium, in China, and at Life Publishers.[30]

By late 1990, the Spanish Edition of the Bible notes was nearing completion. Charles Stewart, the son of an Oklahoma Assemblies of God missionary, was editorial director at Life Publishers and was heavily involved in the Spanish translation:

"We had several cultural problems to deal with. Pentecostals in other parts of the world do not share all of our traditional American beliefs. We had to be sensitive to places in the notes where we felt statements could be misinterpreted or not understood in the Latin American context. We were quick to change the notes to emphasize that, in many cases, there was more than one valid view on a particular subject."[31]

Veteran Missionary Floyd Woodworth and David Gomez-Ruiz played major roles in the Spanish translation of the New Testament notes, which were published in the summer of 1991.

Life Publishers turned to missionaries in foreign countries to help sort out the cultural differences that would have a major impact on the acceptance or rejection of *The Full Life Study Bible*. The foreign missions field directors were added to the special Bible committee and provided invaluable assistance to the foreign language translation process.

Joseph W. Kilpatrick—then at Life Publishers and now general manager of Gospel Publishing House—began the massive task of lining up translators, editors, reviewers, and typesetters. In late 1990 and early 1991, he traveled extensively to the USSR, France, Brazil, Hong Kong, and Korea. Pastor Yonggi Cho in Seoul, Korea, had significant input into the selection of translators for the Korean edition. Brazilian Assemblies of God leader Antonio Gilberto, along with Gordon Chown and Beth Kinas Said, worked on the Portuguese translation.

The new freedom in the former Soviet Union opened doors for Kilpatrick that had not been open since the rise of communism. He met in Moscow for several days with Area Director Robert Mackish and Pentecostal leaders from both Russia and the Ukraine. Life Publishers signed an agreement with the Russian Pentecostal Union for the sales, warehousing, and distribution of the FLSB New Testament. It was a momentous day!

Life Publishers accepted the responsibility for translating, editing, publishing, and shipping the Bibles into Russia. The Pentecostal Union promised to distribute the Bibles and use the profits to buy more Bibles and promote further distribution.

PUSH BACK THE
DARKNESS

❦ *Chapter 13* ❧

Faithful
to the End

One of the most significant statements in the Bible is that of Jesus Christ himself, who said from the cross, "It is finished!" (John 19:30). There is a time to begin, and a time to finish.

In early 1990, Don and Linda bought 160 acres just northwest of Oklahoma City. There was no house on the land, and they didn't have time or money to build; so they moved an old house onto the property. Men from Cornerstone Assembly of God in Oklahoma City and Broken Arrow Assembly of God helped get the house in shape. Don had always loved open spaces and animals, and the acreage was perfect. It was outside the city and provided a conducive atmosphere for writing his study notes.

THE FIRST WARNING

In June, Don mentioned to Linda that his stomach hurt when he ate. He put off a visit to the doctor until after the family returned from a three-week trip to Brazil in July. During the trip he continued to complain about his stomach and his inability to eat as much as usual.

After they returned from Brazil, Don finally made an appointment with Dr. Danny Smith; but by the time he saw Dr. Smith in late September he was unable to eat more than a half plate of food without feeling completely full. Dr. Smith took a biopsy of Don's stomach. It came back negative for cancer but Dr. Smith indicated that Don's stomach was so irritated it looked like hamburger meat.

The doctor prescribed powerful medicine for acute gastritis. Don faithfully took the medication for two months without any improvement.[1]

By Thanksgiving, Don and Linda knew something more had to be done. They scheduled a visit with Dr. Smith and his associate, Dr. Richard Welch. The doctors scoped Don again and decided to go deeper into the lining of the stomach for a biopsy sample. They did the procedure on Friday and told Don the results of the test would be available Monday.

THE CRISIS

On Monday morning, December 3, Linda was talking with a plumber in the kitchen when the phone rang. Don answered the phone in his office.

Linda noticed Don was acting very subdued while the plumber was completing his work on the dishwasher. When the repairman left, Don told Linda, "We have a problem. That was Dr. Smith. I have cancer."

It was a real bombshell.

Linda was in shock.

Dr. Smith told them that immediate stomach surgery was necessary, and they made an appointment with surgeon Robert Arnold, Jr., for the next morning.

Don called his parents, Loren Triplett, Wesley Adams, and Dave Harrison in Brazil and asked them to intercede with God on his behalf.

The next morning Don and Linda and Don's parents met with Dr. Arnold, who explained that the cancer in Don's stomach would have to be removed and that the severity of the problem would not be known until the actual surgery.

Dr. Arnold was very straightforward and pulled no punches in explaining the seriousness of the situation. He scheduled the surgery at Baptist Medical Center in Oklahoma City three days later, December 7.

Don continued calling friends and family members to ask for their prayers. He believed strongly that God had the power to heal him completely.

U.S. Grant called upon Evangelist Ossie B. Jones to pray for Don. Brother Jones was called to preach at age fourteen and had learned "how to preach" from Pastor Grant. Jones was known across the country as an intercessory prayer warrior. Many ministers had looked to him for special prayer through the years. As he prayed, he felt God calling him to pray for Don one hour each day. Don and Brother Jones would become very close over the next eleven months.[2]

The diagnosis of cancer was really no surprise to Don. For months he had known something was terribly wrong with his stomach. The surgery began at six o'clock that afternoon, and the waiting room was packed with Don's and Linda's families, friends, Pastor David Brooks, and Oklahoma District Assemblies of God Missions Director Lindell Warren. After two hours of surgery, Dr. Arnold emerged from the operating room to report that he had removed all of Don's stomach, his spleen, and half of his pancreas. As Don was sent to intensive care, Rev. Warren asked all the family and friends in the waiting room to join hands and pray.

Linda and Don's parents met with Dr. Arnold early the next morning. The news was not good. They had found cancer throughout Don's stomach and adjacent organs. He predicted Don could not live more than a year and a half to two years.

Linda went to the intensive care unit where Don was coming out of the anesthesia.

Don's first question was, "How much time do I have?"

Linda had not planned to tell him his true condition yet, but she felt she had to respond to his question. The hardest thing she ever did in her life was to tell him what Dr. Arnold had said.

Don said, "That will give me time to finish the Old Testament notes."

The next hardest thing was to tell the children.

Toby and Todd—students at Central Bible College— had waited outside; and when Linda told them the devastating news, Todd said, "Well, Mother, God is God! Whether Dad lives or dies, that will not change what I think about God." Don's efforts to establish the idea of the supremacy of God in his children had been successful.

Ossie Jones called Linda for a report on the surgery, and she sobbed as she told him the gloomy news.

Don stayed in the hospital for ten days while doctors decided whether radiation or chemotherapy should be recommended. Later, they sent him home because he was doing surprisingly well following the major surgery. Dr. Arnold had used tissue to form a small pouch to serve as a stomach; yet Don could only eat very small portions of food at a time.

THE WORK GOES ON

The doctors decided on both radiation and chemotherapy treatments, so in early January, 1991, Don and Linda went to M.D. Anderson Hospital in Houston, Texas—a hospital famous for cancer treatment. For the first few days they stayed in a hotel.

212

Zondervan editor Verlyn Verbrugge flew to Houston and spent a weekend with Don going over a list of potential articles for the Old Testament and reviewing completed study notes. From that time on, he began spending more time coordinating the project. He even took Don's notes and put together some of the Old Testament articles. Wesley Adams played an even larger role in editing the notes. Dr. Stanley Horton wrote the notes on the Song of Solomon, Zechariah, and Ecclesiastes; and Don later edited them.

Even though Don was weak, he and Linda continued to work on the study notes. In late January they rented an apartment near the Houston hospital and moved their computer and part of Don's library to the apartment. Don worked two hours each morning on his notes for Isaiah and received his radiation and chemotherapy treatments in the afternoons.

Missionary Gary Davidson learned of Don's illness and flew from Ireland to Houston to visit him. Davidson described his visit:

"He was waiting for me when I got off the plane. Here was a man who had been so healthy and full of life. Now he had lost weight, looked emaciated, and had a cap on his head because the chemotherapy and radiation treatments had made him lose some of his hair. It was very emotional. We spent the entire next day reminiscing, singing, and worshipping together. Our people in Ireland began immediately to fast and pray for Don's healing."[3]

Don and Linda flew home to Oklahoma City each weekend to spend time with the children. Toby and Todd had left Central Bible College in Springfield, Missouri, to spend that year with their father during his illness. They took care of Tiffany during the week, and all awaited expectantly for their parents to come home on the weekends.

SPIRITUAL WARFARE WITH THE DARKNESS

In March, Don's treatments ended and he and Linda moved back home to the farm. Don continued to believe God was able to heal him. Thousands of people around the world prayed for his healing. He talked to Ossie Jones five or six times a week; and Brother Jones fervently prayed that God would allow him to complete the Old Testament notes.

One morning, Don said, "I can't do it anymore! I'll ask Doctor Horton to finish the notes."

Linda called Ossie Jones, who talked to Don and asked him bluntly, "Who did God call to write this study Bible?"

Don was silent. Then, weak and wane as he was, Don began weeping.

Ossie Jones prayed with him for fifteen minutes.

Abruptly, Don ended the conversation by saying, "Brother Jones, Brother Jones, I've got to go! I've got to start writing!"[4]

THE COST OF PENTECOST

It is a seldom considered fact that many of the people who were filled with the Holy Spirit and spoke in other tongues at Pentecost ultimately gave their lives for the cause of Christ. The Spirit-filled life goes far beyond the joy of miracles and blessing in church services to apply the source of that joy to practical Christian service—and it is there in the crucible of suffering that the greatest work of the Spirit-anointed servant is accomplished. The task is spiritual and must be carried out in the realm of the Spirit.

A woman in Wesley Adams' congregation in Kansas City had two visions about Don and *The Full Life Study Bible*. She saw him and his family in a foxhole fighting the satanic principalities in Brazil. Their backs were unguarded, and they were being attacked by lesser demonic forces, one of which was cancer. She then saw a man come to stand back to back with Don and fight off the attacks from the rear. That person no doubt was Ossie Jones.

In the second vision, the woman saw Brazil as if it were covered with a brass dome, which she interpreted as the darkness of Roman Catholicism and spiritism that hovers over that country. She then saw a small opening occur in the top of the brass dome. *The Full Life Study Bible* came tumbling from heaven, went through the hole in the brass covering, and caused a tremendous explosion in Brazil.

The visions alerted Don and Wesley to the enormous backlash they were receiving from the opposing powers of darkness and the magnitude of spiritual warfare that was occurring in connection with the project. It was during that same period that Wesley's wife, Jane, lost function of both of her kidneys before a successful transplant.[5]

THE VIA DOLOROSA—THE WAY OF SUFFERING

The physical manifestation of spiritual warfare came as a surprise to Don and his family and friends. Yet, most men and women who have accomplished anything great for God have had to face the opposition of evil. It generally does not come by an obviously supernatural manifestation such as might frighten or intimidate those of lesser spiritual maturity but rather by a tightening of circumstances, a prolonged period of struggle, of financial difficulties, or of health problems that threaten life itself. Don Stamps had experienced

215

such a period in western Kansas before returning to Brazil; and when it appeared that he would go back to Brazil to accomplish his great life's work, Linda lost her finger in a freak accident.

It is not a matter of superstition or even of fear, for the man or woman of God knows the admonishment of Jesus Christ in John 16:33—"In this world you have tribulation, but take courage; I have overcome the world." *The Full Life Study Bible* was and continues to be a powerful attack on the darkness of this world; and such warfare cannot be waged without suffering the onslaught of the enemy of our souls.

It was not that Don Stamps did not understand this principle, for in his own notes he wrote concerning Acts 28:16 [Bible book abbreviations those of Zondervan Publishing House]: "It had been Paul's desire to preach the gospel in Rome (Ro 15:22-29) and it was also God's will that he do so (23:11). Yet Paul arrived in Rome in chains and only after setbacks, storms, shipwreck, and many trials. Though Paul remained faithful, God did not make his way easy and trouble free. Likewise, we may be in God's will and entirely faithful to him; nevertheless, he may direct us in unpleasant paths involving troubles. Yet we can know that 'in all things God works for the good of those who love him' (Ro 8:28)."

Yes, Don Stamps understood the price for doing great good in an evil world. His greatest concern was not for himself but for the completion of his divinely ordained task. He wrote a beautiful treatise on suffering after reading 1 Peter 2:20-21—"But if you suffer for doing good and you endure it, this is commendable before God. To this you were called, because Christ suffered for you, leaving you an example, that you should follow in his steps."

Don wrote in his Bible notes, "The highest glory and privilege of any believer is to suffer for Christ and the gospel. In suffering, believers follow the example of Christ and the apostles (Isa 53; Mt 16:21; 20:28; Ac 9:16, note; Heb 5:8). (1) Christians must be willing to suffer (4:1; 2Co 11:23), i.e., to share in the sufferings of Christ (4:13; 2Co 1:5; Php 3:10), and expect suffering to be a part of their ministry (1Co 11:1; 2Co 4:10-12). (2) Suffering for Christ is called suffering 'according to God's will' (4:19), for his 'name' (Ac 9:16), 'for the gospel' (2Ti 1:8), 'for what is right' (3:14) and for 'the kingdom of God' (2Th 1:5). (3) Suffering for Christ is a way to arrive at spiritual maturity (Heb 2:10), to obtain God's blessing (4:14) and to minister life to others (2Co 4:10-12). Sharing in Christ's suffering is a prerequisite for being glorified with Christ (Ro 8:17) and attaining eternal glory (Ro 8:18). In this sense it may be regarded as a precious gift from God (vs. 19; Php 1:29). (4) In living for Christ and the gospel, suffering should not be sought, but believers must be willing to undergo it out of devotion to Christ."

In most cases, spiritual storms will pass. The Christian holds steady, remains faithful, and realizes that as Christ suffered the most during His greatest work on Calvary so His followers will carry out their most effective spiritual work at a price of suffering. And even if no relief comes, the greatest honor of any Christian is to die in His service. It is the Via Dolorosa—the Way of Suffering.

Death for Don Stamps was a victory, not a defeat. He asked only that he might finish the notes to *The Full Life Study Bible*—a goal that he attained.

THE BEGINNING OF THE END

Throughout March and April, Don worked hard on the notes. Miraculously, he felt reasonably well; and he and Linda could spend up to five or six hours a day writing and editing.

In May, Don began vomiting bile.

Dr. Arnold diagnosed the problem as an inflamed gall bladder, and a few days later he removed it. But Don continued to vomit. Another round of x-rays at Baptist Medical Center revealed that the cancer was blocking his intestines. Dr. Arnold again performed surgery but could not remove the cancer.

Don and Linda both knew it was the beginning of the end. Linda was physically and mentally worn out from the months of caring for Don. Her hopes had been buoyed by his two good months in March and April; but now she was drained, and only the prayers of friends and strangers in places she had never heard of kept her going.

Don never became bitter. He viewed the cancer as a blow from the enemy, but continued to do all he knew to do—trust God and submit to His sovereignty. At times he cried when he realized he was probably going to leave his family.

THE SUPPORT OF FRIENDS

Don Stamps had made a thousand friends in his half century on earth; and most of them showed up at the farm in the summer of 1991. Don visited every few days by phone with Wesley Adams. He shared with Loren Rovenstine that he knew the devil would be happy if he denied Jesus because of his illness and assured Loren that such would not happen. He confided in Gary Davidson that he could not have enough faith for his own healing and needed the continuing prayers of believers everywhere. He told Gary he did not understand why he was getting worse. He knew it was not from God but was an attack of Satan. He was convinced that Satan did not want the notes to *The Full Life Study Bible* completed and that the spiritual warfare over his life was tremendous.

Letters of prayer and support from friends and pastors like David Wilkerson came daily. Loren Triplett and the Assemblies of God Headquarters in Springfield initiated prayer meetings among missionaries around the globe.

Dave Harrison called Don daily during his last months. They prayed and cried together. One day, Don stopped Dave and said, "What do you want me to tell Dee Dee [the daughter the Harrisons had lost in Brazil] when I see her?" Dave knew Don was expecting to die and see Dee Dee in heaven.[6]

In August, Don wanted the whole family to go to Colorado. He was really in no shape to go. He had lost 40 pounds and weighed only 130. His parents and Linda, Toby, Todd, and Tiffany loaded up in two cars and drove two days to Buena Vista, Colorado. Don was weak but managed to fish a little for a few days.

Lawrence Williams talked to Don many times during the last few months. Don bared his soul to Lawrence. He was discouraged and did not understand why this terrible thing was happening to him. Dave Harrison came for a visit. He, Lawrence, and Don rode around in the car for hours talking about Don's frustration with the situation.[7]

Linda would later say as she spoke at the Division of Foreign Missions Fly-Ins in 1994:

"By this time Don was in a very weakened condition. He had been six feet tall and weighed one hundred eighty pounds. Now he was bent over and weighed barely one hundred pounds. He had aged twenty years in six short months. Sometimes he could only work an hour a day, and the day that he wrote that last note in the Old Testament he vomited bile all day long.

"What would make a man spend nine years of his life working day after day, month after month, and year after year, in research and writing? What would push a man to keep writing while he spent the last eleven months of his life sick with cancer, a pump at one side of his desk pumping liquid food through his feeding tube and a large plastic waste basket on the other side of his desk so that he could spit out the bile that continued to rise from his cancerous digestive system? What would make him stay at that desk until he finished notes for *The Full Life Study Bible*? I believe the main reason was the call of God on his life to the country of Brazil."[8]

THE PRAYING STOPPED

In the last week of September, Ossie Jones called Don with a startling revelation. He said, "Don, God told me to stop praying for you last night. My burden to pray for you every day has been lifted."

Don replied, "I finished my notes on the Old Testament yesterday."

Ossie Jones then realized that his prayer burden for ten months had not been for Don's healing but for Don to have the strength to finish the notes for *The Full Life Study Bible*.[9]

On the day Don completed the notes on Malachi, the last book in the Old Testament, he vomited bile all day long.

He and Linda packaged up the last set of notes and sent them to Verlyn Verbrugge for editing.

The last notes Don wrote were for the final verse in Malachi (4:6)—"And he will restore the hearts of the fathers to their children, and the hearts of the children to their fathers, lest I come and smite the land with a curse."

Don wrote of that verse:

"The future ministry of the coming prophet is described in terms of putting families right with God and each other. John the Baptist preached to this end (see Luke 1:17). (1) There can be no blessing from God or abundant life in the Spirit if God's people do not make family authority, love, and faithfulness absolute priorities in the church. The purity and righteousness of the home must be maintained or our congregations will fail.

"(2) The one most responsible for accomplishing this task is the father of the family. Fathers must love their children by praying for them (see John 17:1, note), spending time with them, pointing out the ungodly ways of the world, and diligently teaching them God's Word and righteous standards....

"(3) Pastors must also make this goal of John the Baptist their own purpose for their ministry, thus preparing the church for the Lord's coming (see Luke 1:17, note)."[10]

The Bible notes were finished.

A MARVELOUS TESTIMONY

A beautiful Christian testimony has come to light that occurred shortly after the publishers released *The Full Life Study Bible*. Gospel Publishing House was promoting the new Pentecostal study Bible at the April, 1993, National

Light-for-the-Lost Convention in Oklahoma City when a woman approached the book exhibit and told her story. Here is that story as Linda Stamps told it in later presentations:

"I was not involved in the selling, but my friend Bob Burke was helping GPH. After one of the evening services, he came up to me and said, 'Linda, let me tell you what a lady told me today. She came up to the booth, and I was getting ready to sell her a Bible when she stopped me and said, 'Just a minute, Young Man, I want to tell you a story about the Full Life Study Bible.'

"She said that for years she and her husband had had a very troubled marriage. They had two children, and by the time they were teenagers they had caused them a lot of heartache and sorrow. Finally, the youngest child had finished high school, and they had all decided that after Christmas all four were going to go their separate ways.

"'But,' she said, 'for Christmas my mother gave me a Full Life Study Bible. And since Christmas is the time for families, we decided that we would like to try one more time to keep our family together. We knew if we were going to succeed we would have to start having family devotions. The first day we sat down to have our devotions together I took my new Full Life Study Bible and turned to the Book of Malachi.'

"I looked at my friend Bob and kind of laughed. I asked, 'Bob, are you sure she said Malachi? If I had those kinds of problems I don't think I would turn to that last book!' Then I remembered that the last verse in the Old Testament talks about the hearts of the children being restored to the fathers and the hearts of the fathers to their children. The woman said she read that verse and then looked down to see if the author of the study notes had written on that verse, and he had. She read it aloud to her family, and the Holy Spirit used those words to begin melting the ice that had been around their hearts for so long.

"To make a long story short, she said they began to really communicate for the first time in years. They all four rededicated their lives to the Lord. Today, they are together as a family, and they use their Full Life Study Bible every day."[11]

Perhaps Loren Triplett expressed best the gratitude of unknown millions when he wrote to Don:

"Let me seek to express my deepest admiration and appreciation for the obedience with which you proceeded year after year with the vision you received from the Lord of the harvest. You have provided light for the pathways of millions of believers, and I choose to believe firmly that its effective influence will continue until Jesus comes."[12]

THE LAST DAYS

In early October, Don wanted to see the farm at Goodland one more time. Toby and Todd prepared a bed in the back of the station wagon for the long trip to western Kansas. He visited for the last time with old friends like Bob Silkman and saw the old farm.

The pain was almost unbearable. Linda had to get up every two hours during the night to administer strong pain medication. The boys alternated staying up with Don, who was so weak he needed help to get to his bed. He was losing weight daily and now was down to 100 pounds.

Don's old college buddy Larry Fine came for a last visit:

"At our last meeting together, I took Don riding around. He said he was not at all mad at God or scared to die. We talked about the fun stories of our past. We talked about how Don was always a fighter.... For Don there was no gray on any issue. He was driven always, right up to his very own death. As I prepared to leave, Don walked over and gave me a big hug. I knew it would be our last.

"I talked with him on the phone a few days before he died. I could tell he was in pain. His speech was weak. I told him to tell my dad hello and that I would be there someday. His last words were, 'I'm gonna go find us a trout stream.' He always had faith in God and never became angered about his untimely illness. There was no bitterness at all."[13]

Don and Linda talked about the end. Don did not want to die at home. Toby told his mother that God had given him a peace about his dad, and God gave that same peace to Linda. The Lord was preparing the Stamps family for Don's death.

His body was racked with pain. Linda sat up with him all Monday night, November 4. The pain medicine was not working at all. On Tuesday morning, they looked at each other and knew it was time to go to the hospital. They went to the doctor, who agreed that Don was in his final days.

Don wanted to wait a few hours before entering the hospital, so they went back home. He called Wesley Adams and said goodbye. He called his parents and told them how much he loved them. He asked the boys to take him around the farm for one last look. He gathered Linda, the boys, and Tiffany around him. They hugged and cried and prayed.

Then they went to the hospital.

FAREWELL

The hospital provided a suite for Don so Linda or the boys could stay all night with him. His parents and brothers David and Bobby, Linda's parents and her sister, Paula

Anderson and her husband Don, and nieces and nephews all gathered in the hospital room. Don sat in a wheelchair and enjoyed the storytelling, laughing, and joking. Both he and Linda slept well the first night. The pain medication allowed Don to sleep most of the next day.

The second night in the hospital was difficult. Toby and Linda sat up with Don all night as he vomited continually.

The next morning Linda had a beauty shop appointment. While she was there, the phone rang. Linda's mother was at the hospital and told her to come quickly because the nurse had said Don was dying.

Linda rushed to the hospital and took hold of her husband's hand. His eyes were closed but he squeezed her hand when she talked to him.

A few minutes later Todd came to his father's bedside and said, "Dad, this is Todd. Can you hear me?"

Don gave a slight nod of his head.

Ten minutes later, on November 7, 1991, Don C. Stamps went to be with the Lord he had served. It was only three days before his 53rd birthday.

Toby and Todd had been at Linda's side when Don passed away, but Tiffany had been in school. Tiffany was 14, and she and her father had been very close. Linda was concerned about how she would react to the death of her father. Many tears flowed at home that afternoon when the four of them were reunited.

Later that evening, Linda's sister Paula Anderson came out to spend the night with them. They were all in the living room talking when Linda noticed that Tiffany had left the room. She said to her sister, "Paula, Tiffany has probably gone to her room to cry. I need to go check on her."

As Linda walked down the hall toward Tiffany's bedroom, she listened for sounds of sobbing but did not hear any. When she got to the bedroom door, it was closed. She stopped a moment to listen, but it was quiet inside. She opened the door and went into the dark room. As she got closer to the bed, she could tell that Tiffany was not asleep. Linda sat down on the edge of the bed and asked, "Tiffany Honey, what are you doing?"

Tiffany said, "Well, Mother, I'm just lying here thinking about how much fun Daddy must be having in heaven. He's already seen Jesus, and probably tomorrow he's going to get to go fishing."

Don loved to fish. As the tears rolled down Linda's cheeks, she thanked God for His plan of salvation. "Thank you, Lord Jesus. Only a fourteen-year-old girl who knows you as her personal Savior can have that kind of hope of eternal life and know that one day she will see her daddy again."

THE FUNERAL

Don had wanted so much to go back to Brazil. He wanted to stay and fight the devil everywhere he could. In Brazil, he wanted to seek the Lord's enablement to do four things: (1) preach the gospel and evangelize; (2) lead people into the baptism in the Holy Spirit; (3) see the sick miraculously healed; and, (4) cast out demons. Don's intense study of New Testament apostolic Christianity created a desire to see it in his own ministry. He wanted to live the life and ministry that he wrote about in *The Full Life Study Bible*.[14]

A few days before he died, Don had asked his pastor, David Brooks, to promise that no one would be allowed to touch his body for fifteen minutes after death. He told Pastor

Brooks, "I want to try to talk the Lord into letting me come back."[15]

Hundreds of people attended the funeral on November 11 at Cornerstone Assembly of God in Oklahoma City. The service was a glorious worship service, just as Don had requested. Friends and co-workers came from as far away as Brazil for the service.

Loren Triplett lauded Don and Linda's devotion to the completion of the study Bible project:

"I had a wonderful experience early this morning as I turned to the last pages of the Old Testament and tried to understand the ecstasy that Don must have felt only a few weeks ago upon completion of this work. These were the last words that Don wrote and handed to Linda to enter into the computer for all the world to see—'And He will turn the hearts of the fathers to their children, and the hearts of the children to their fathers' [KJV]. Toby, Todd, and Tiffany, God bless you! The whole world wishes me to thank you four today for your unswerving devotion to this project. Don, thank you for your love for the eternal Word of God. Thank you for your holy intensity, your practical theology, and the tough tenacity you drew upon to finish your work. You have left a deeper impression in your fifty-three years than most of us would in a hundred years."[16]

Don had asked his dearest and best friend, Wesley Adams, to preach his funeral message. From his wheelchair, Wesley said farewell to Don:

"Today there is sorrow over what some would call the premature passing of our friend. But I feel great comfort and joy in knowing that Don is with the Lord. He has been taken away from evil. His suffering is over forever. And he has completed the race successfully. He has taken a drink from the crystal clear water of life that flows from the throne of God and runs now through the middle of the great city of Heaven.

"He has taken from the fruit of the tree of life, and he has eaten and is full and satisfied today. For over a month he was unable to eat food or drink water at the end of his life. He mentioned to me many times how thirsty he was and how the first thing he would ask the Lord for was a drink of water. He now drinks from that water that satisfies the deepest thirst and eats from that tree that provides eternal life.

"Don was a mighty warrior and strategist, always think-ing of a way to do it better. And he fell while fighting in the trenches. His faith in God remained unshaken to the very end. There is clearly a part that we don't understand in this hour. Don knows and understands it a whole lot more clearly than we do right now.

"I was confident that God would heal Don because tens of thousands around the world were praying for him. When I got the news of his death, I wondered about the interces-sion. The Holy Spirit whispered in my ear, 'None of those prayers are wasted.' A flood of intercession went up for Don. I believe God has collected those prayers in a bowl in Heaven, and while God in his wisdom has chosen not to pour them out upon Don, God is going to take those prayers and will pour them out in His time. The prayers for heal-ing are going to be released on the earth. The prayers for deliverance will be released and hundreds of thousands of captives will be set free in part because of the intercession for Don. Isaiah 43:4-6 says, 'I will give other men in your place and other peoples in exchange for your life.... I will bring your offspring from the east and gather you from the west. I will say to the north, 'Give them up!' And to the south, 'Do not hold them back.' Bring My sons from afar, and My daughters from the ends of the earth' When we sit down at the great banquet at the end of history, I believe there will come those from all over the earth and they will be offspring that will testify to the righteous influence of Don Stamps."[17]

U.S. Grant closed the funeral with prayer:

"Dear Father, I want to thank you for bringing Don Stamps into my life. I thank you because we know where he is today. The last time any of us saw him, he had his face set toward home. You taught him to live victoriously, even through suffering. You gave him a triumphant passing into the everlasting Kingdom. I believe that from the foundations of this earth, you mapped out the ministry of Don Stamps."[18]

One of the greatest tributes to Don's life was manifested in the life of his old teenage friend, David Fine. David had drifted from God but was so moved at the funeral that he rededicated his life to God and is now an active church member. Just a few weeks before his death Don told David that he needed to "get his act straight" so they could spend eternity together in heaven. David said, "I didn't know what we had had until we lost Don. I count myself lucky to have even known Don Stamps in this life. He was never dull. He made life worth living."[19]

Why did God allow Don Stamps to be stricken with fatal cancer at such a young age? It is a question that will never be adequately answered this side of heaven. U.S. Grant has an opinion:

"We want to fit God into our premise. He won't fit. He does what He wants to do, the way He wants to do it. If you are building an edifice, there are certain tools you use. When you are finished, you lay them aside. Each set of tools is for a specific task. Jesus is building his Church. When He has used a specific person, or tool, He lays him aside, says thank you, and goes on with His building."[20]

Dr. Stanley Horton said:

"To be present with the Lord is far better than this life on earth. This body is a temporary house. I saw in Don that while the outward man was perishing, the inward man was being renewed constantly."[21]

Ossie Jones said, "Don received his healing. It is now eternal."[22]

Loren Triplett said, "His work was finished. His legacy and his life live on. In some strange way his death contributes to the massive worldwide distribution of *The Full Life Study Bible* so dear to his heart."[23]

The story of David's death in the Bible may best explain why Don Stamps left this earth prematurely. "For David, after he had served the purpose of God in his own generation, fell asleep" (Acts 13:36).

PUSH BACK THE
DARKNESS

∽ *Chapter 14* ∾

God's Word
Is My Final
Authority

Zondervan Publishing House released the English edition of the complete *Full Life Study Bible* on September 1, 1992. This Bible is a clear call for Christians to return to a highway of holiness (Isa. 35:8) and sounds the opening trumpet of a worldwide end-time revival of the Holy Spirit (Joel 2:28-32). That's exactly what Don Stamps wanted the Bible notes to be.

Over the following years, Linda Stamps threw herself into promoting the new Bible and dedicated all the earnings to the Assemblies of God Division of Foreign Missions for the translation of the notes into other Bibles around the world.

At the time of this writing, the notes are being translated into sixteen major languages of the world, with many more translations being planned for the future. The Assemblies of God, the Church of God (Cleveland, Tennessee), the Church of God in Christ, the Pentecostal Church of God, the Pentecostal Assemblies of Canada, and other Pentecostal denominations have officially endorsed the Bible and are promoting its distribution.

Loren Triplett calls the Bible "a last day missionary project with world influence, an anchor, a guideline, the road to run a revival on. It is what we believe, it is said simply, and in the right place, at the foot of the pages of the Holy Bible."[1]

Dr. Yonggi Cho, pastor of Yoido Full Gospel Church in Seoul, Korea, says, "This Bible repeatedly emphasizes the absolute priority of New Testament truth."[2]

David Wilkerson believes the Bible comes at "just the right time to strengthen the roots of evangelical Christianity."[3]

Missionary to Ireland Gary Davidson said, "Don was a voice in the wilderness that none of us had heard. He reminded us of the cost paid by our forefathers. His legacy is left in the Bible he gave us. His death galvanized our commitment as missionaries and preachers. This Bible was his goal and he finished the course."[4]

Dave Harrison's hope is that the Bible will "preserve the fruits of Pentecost and the holiness doctrine."[5]

Dr. Stanley Horton's prayer is that *The Full Life Study Bible* will bring "a revival of holiness" because "if the Pentecostal and charismatic movements do not have a revival of holiness, they will gradually lose their power."[6]

Dr. William Menzies describes the Bible as "a volume that articulates the basic theological positions held by the vast majority of Pentecostals." Dr. Menzies hopes the Bible will "provide theological stability for the Pentecostal revival around the world."[7]

Missionary Rick Hoover says that when the study notes are published in Portuguese, the Bible will sweep Brazil because "there will be a committed corps of missionaries to promote the Bible from the *Oiapoque ao Chui*, a Brazilian expression that refers to the northernmost and southernmost points of Brazil."[8]

Joseph W. Kilpatrick, now the national director of the Division of Publication for the Assemblies of God and general manager of the Gospel Publishing House, sees the Bible as "becoming a worldwide standard of faith and practice for Pentecostals."[9]

Seventy-seven articles on subjects ranging from creation to Christ's message to the seven churches appear in *The Full Life Study Bible*. The theme of the absolute inerrancy of the Bible is found from Genesis to Revelation. Here is a sample of Don's notes:

"Scripture is the very life and Word of God. Down to the very words of the original manuscripts, the Bible is without error, absolutely true, trustworthy, and infallible. To deny the full inspiration of the holy Scripture, therefore, is to set aside the fundamental witness of Jesus Christ, the Holy Spirit, and the apostles. Furthermore, to limit or disregard its inerrancy is to impair its divine authority."[10]

Don's strong belief that ministers must live a godly and morally blameless life comes through loud and clear:

"Any professed call of God to do the work of a pastor must be tested by the members of the church according to the biblical standards.... The church must not endorse any person for the ministerial work based solely on his desire, education, burden, or alleged vision or call. The church today has no right to diminish the requirements that God has set forth by the Holy Spirit. They stand as absolutes and must be followed for the sake of God's name, His kingdom, and the credibility of the high office of overseer.... Today's churches must not turn from the righteous requirements for an overseer set forth by God in the original revelation of the apostles. Instead, the church must require from its leaders the highest standard of holiness, perseverance in faithfulness to God and his Word, and godly living.... To throw aside the principle of having godly leadership that has set an unblemished pattern for those of the church to follow is to ignore Scripture's clear teaching."[11]

The Full Life Study Bible emphasizes the importance of strong family relationships:

"It is the responsibility of parents to give their children the upbringing that prepares them for lives pleasing to God. It is the family, not the church or church school, that is primarily responsible for the biblical and spiritual training of the children.... The very core of Christian nurture is this: The heart of the father must be turned to the heart of the child in order to bring the heart of the child to the heart of the Savior."[12]

Don's own family life was a blueprint for his notes on Christian families. In the summer of 1982 he sent a tape letter to Wesley Adams:

"It's almost midnight now. We just had a prayer meeting, my two boys, Tiffany, Linda and me. What a blessed time! We laid hands on each other, represented those we feel who are lost in our families. I don't ever remember holding my two boys and weeping as I did tonight. We prayed that we would stick together for Jesus until the day we all died. We all wept and cried. What a great night this has been with the Lord!"[13]

Don's last notes on the Old Testament echoed the call for strong Christian families:

"There can be no blessing from God or abundant life in the Spirit if God's people do not make family authority, love, and faithfulness absolute priorities in the church. The purity and righteousness of the home must be maintained or our congregations will fail."[14]

The Holy Spirit played an important role in the life of Don Stamps. His desire for a deeper experience led him to U.S. Grant's office where he and Wesley received the baptism in the Holy Spirit. The speaking in tongues issue caused him to leave Brazil as a Nazarene missionary and ultimately led to his acceptance by the Assemblies of God. Naturally, he emphasized the biblical teaching about the Holy Spirit as a prominent theme in his New Testament notes:

"It is essential that believers recognize the importance of the Holy Spirit in God's redemptive purpose. Many Christians have no idea what difference it would make if there were no Holy Spirit in this world. Without the Holy Spirit there would be no creation, no universe, no human race. Without the Holy Spirit there would be no Bible, no New Testament, no power to proclaim the gospel. Without the Holy Spirit there would be no faith, no new birth, no holiness, no Christians."[15]

On the significance of speaking in tongues, he wrote:

"Speaking in tongues, or glossolalia, was considered by the New Testament Christians as a God-given sign accompanying the baptism in the Holy Spirit.... This Biblical pattern for the Spirit-filled life is still valid for us today.... God linked speaking in tongues with the baptism in the Spirit from the very beginning so that the 120 believers at Pentecost and believers thereafter would have an experiential confirmation that they had received the baptism.... Throughout the history of the church, whenever tongues as a confirming sign has been denied or lost from view, the truth and experience of Pentecost has been distorted or ignored entirely."[16]

One of his goals in writing the study notes was to stop what he called the "erosion of our old-fashioned Pentecostal beliefs." He saw Pentecostals in America leaving their holiness roots:

"We need to admit and recognize that within the Pentecostal movement there is now occurring a slow process of departure from our unique, historic, theological heritage. We have departed from a life based on Christlikeness and biblical righteousness. If this process continues, it will only be a matter of time until our place of election in the history of redemption will be in grave peril.... The Pentecostal faith and movement cannot endure unless it is based on the foundational pillars of truth and righteousness. The 'truth' involves commitment to the fundamentals of faith, i.e. complete inerrancy of Scripture, salvation by faith in Christ and His blood atonement, the virgin birth, the bodily resurrection of Christ, the scriptural doctrine of sin, the return of Christ for His church, etc. The 'righteousness' involves a clear separation from the ways of the world and a seeking of godliness in all our ways. We must see again, as did the first Pentecostals of this century, that the Holy Spirit who fills us with His presence is first and foremost a 'Spirit of holiness' who leads us into all the truth.... We must understand that contending for the faith is not an option, but a matter of life and death. The eternal destiny of the souls of many will be determined by our devotion or lack of devotion to the Pentecostal faith committed to us."[17]

Don preached his last sermon to the student body of Central Bible College in Springfield, Missouri. He challenged them with his fervor for a Pentecostal revival:

"We have the only fully adequate message that is going to reach this world. Don't lose faith in it. Contend for it. Believe in it one-hundred percent. Go forth into this world. Realize that the same promise Christ made to the disciples is true for us. We claim our inheritance. God can do in your life and the lives of our congregations the same thing He did in the Book of Acts."[18]

When his life's work was done, Don Stamps set aside his last yellow pad, put down his favorite ballpoint pen, and soon departed from us. Like Enoch of old, he "walked with God; and he was not, for God took him" (Gen. 5:24). In spite of all his troubled youth and misunderstood adult life, the Lord's grace and the deep exposure to the Word of God transformed him into spiritual greatness.

Since his death, Linda has excelled in her own way by giving her testimony and offering *The Full Life Study Bible* in churches and conferences across the nation. Toby, Todd, and Tiffany are all serving the Lord; and Don's inspired notes are being translated and printed in the Bibles of many nations. There is no way to measure the whole effect, but it is certain that millions of people will gather around the throne of God in heaven because of one man's holy dedication to God and His Word. As Don loved to say, "God's Word is my final authority!"

— Endnotes —

CHAPTER 1

1. Letter from Don Stamps to Bob Silkman, May 1982.

2. Published by Zondervan Publishing House in cooperation with Gospel Publishing House and Life Publishers International.

3. This quote and those that follow in this chapter are from Donald C. Stamps' Author's Preface to *The Full Life Study Bible* (Zondervan Bible Publishers, Grand Rapids, Michigan, in cooperation with the Assemblies of God Gospel Publishing House and Life Publishers International). The punctuation, grammatical style, and abbreviations are those of the publisher.

CHAPTER 2

1. L.J. Trinterud, "John Knox," *The World Book Encyclopedia*, 1981, Vol. 11, p. 285.

2. Interview with Woody and Emma Stamps, September 2, 1992. Much of the personal information about Don's early life in this chapter was gleaned from this interview.

3. Tape of sermon by Don Stamps at Evangel Assembly, Wichita, Kansas, June 10, 1979.

4. Interview with David Stamps, September 12, 1992.

CHAPTER 3

1. Interview with Richard Teas, November 15, 1992.

2. Frank Mead, *Handbook of Denominations* (Nashville, Abingdon Press, 1985).

3. Interview with Lowell Reed, October 22, 1992.

4. Tape of sermon by Don Stamps at Evangel Assembly, Wichita, Kansas, June 10, 1979.

5. Interview with Lloyd and Don Plunkett, September 21, 1992.

6. Interview with Wendell Payton, September 22, 1992.

7. Interview with Lloyd Plunkett, September 21, 1992.

8. Interview with Don Plunkett, September 21, 1992.

9. Interview with David Stamps, September 12, 1992.

10. Interview with David Stamps, September 12, 1992.

11. Interview with Jim Dimick, December 3, 1992, and letters from Dimick to author in December 1992 and January 1993. Dimick knew Don Stamps better than anyone during Don's last two years at Bethany Nazarene College. He has keen insight into what experiences formed Don's beliefs and character.

12. Interview with Wilma, David, and John Fine, September 20, 1992.

13. Interview with David Brown, September 21, 1992.

14. Jim Dimick interview.

CHAPTER 4

1. Tape of sermon by Don Stamps, Evangel Assembly, Wichita, Kansas, June 10, 1979.

2. Ruth Tucker, *From Jerusalem to Irian Jaya* (Grand Rapids, Zondervan Publishing House, 1983), p. 147.

3. Timothy L. Smith, *Called Unto Holiness* (Kansas City, Nazarene Publishing House, 1962), pp. 226-227, 326.

4. Smith, Chapter 5.

5. Interview with Larry Fine, September 17, 1992.

6. Interview with Carl Godwin, September 30, 1992, and interview with Charles Pickens, September 18, 1992.

7. Interview with Dan Davis, October 19, 1992.

8. Interview with Dr. Donald Metz, September 21, 1992.

9. Interview with Lawrence Williams, September 8, 1992.

10. Interviews with Linda Stamps, August 12, 1992 and October 26, 1992.

11. Interview with Larry Fine, September 17, 1992.

12. Interview with Jim Dimick, December 3, 1992.

13. Letter from Jim Dimick, January 10, 1993.

14. Letter from Jim Dimick, December 15, 1992.

15. Letter from Jim Dimick, December 31, 1992.

16. Interview with Carl Godwin, September 30, 1992.

CHAPTER 5

1. Interview with Wesley Adams, September 18, 1992.

2. Wesley Adams interview.

3. Interview with Rodger Young, September 21, 1992.

4. Wesley Adams interview.

5. Rodger Young interview.

6. W.J. Hollenweger, *The Pentecostals* (Minneapolis, Augsburg Publishing House, 1972), pp. 75-84.

7. Brazil, "Field Focus," Division of Foreign Missions, The Assemblies of God, Springfield, Missouri, March, 1978.

CHAPTER 6

1. Ralph M. Riggs, *The Spirit Himself* (Springfield, Missouri, Gospel Publishing House, 1949), pp. 47-48.

2. Riggs, p. 50.

3. Riggs, p. 55.

4. Riggs, p. 80.

5. Interview with Wesley Adams, September 18, 1992.

6. Stanley Horton, *What the Bible Says About the Holy Spirit* (Springfield, Gospel Publishing House, 1976), pp. 142, 157.

7. William Menzies, *Anointed to Serve* (Springfield, Gospel Publishing House, 1971), p. 51.

8. Interview with U.S. Grant, July 3, 1992.

9. Interview with Wesley Adams, September 18, 1992.

10. Interview with Linda Stamps, August 12, 1992.

11. The Assemblies of God generally has the same requirement. Since much of the work of foreign missions relates to pastors and local churches, those missionaries who never pastor a church must operate at a distinct disadvantage.

CHAPTER 7

1. *They Came to Stay: A History of Sherman County, Kansas,* Vol. 1, p. 11, Sherman County Historical Society, 1980.

2. *They Came to Stay,* p. 370.

3. Letter from Don Stamps to Wesley Adams, August 15, 1968.

4. Letter from Don Stamps to Wesley Adams, September 1, 1968.

5. Letter from Don Stamps to Wesley Adams, September 8, 1968.

6. Interview with Loren Rovenstine, September 14, 1992.

7. Rovenstine interview.

8. Revival handbill from the files of Don Stamps.

9. Interview with Wesley Adams, September 18, 1992.

10. Interview with Linda Stamps, October 26, 1992.

11. Linda Stamps interview.

12. Wesley Adams interview.

CHAPTER 8

1. Tape of sermon by Don Stamps, Evangel Assembly, Wichita, Kansas, June 10, 1979.

2. Manoel Cardozo, *The World Book Encyclopedia*, 1981, Volume 2, pp. 469-478.

3. Letter from Linda Stamps to Bob and Irma Silkman, February 3, 1971.

4. Interview with Roger Maze, September 10, 1992.

5. Interview with Jim Bond, September 16, 1992.

6. Letter from Don Stamps to Wesley Adams, March 1, 1971.

7. Interview with Linda Stamps, August 12, 1992.

8. Roger Maze interview.

9. Letter from Don Stamps to Wesley Adams, April 17, 1971.

10. April 17, 1971 letter from Stamps to Adams.

11. Letter from Don Stamps to Dr. V.H. Lewis, April, 1971.

12. Letter from Stamps to Lewis.

13. Letter from Don Stamps to Wesley Adams, April 23, 1971.

14. Roger Maze interview.

15. Letter from Wesley Adams to Don Stamps, April 24, 1971.

16. Letter from Don Stamps to Wesley Adams, August 7, 1971.

17. Letter from Don Stamps to Dr. Paul Orjala, November 6, 1971.

18. Interview with Maze and Bond.

19. Letter from Stamps to Orjala.

20. Letter form Stamps to Orjala.

21. Interview with Wesley Adams, September 18, 1992.

22. Bond interview.

23. Maze interview.

24. Letter from Don Stamps to Dr. Everett Phillips, January 28, 1972.

25. Letter from Dr. Everett Phillips to Don Stamps, January 29, 1972.

26. Letter from Don Stamps to Wesley Adams, January 30, 1972.

CHAPTER 9

1. Interview with Linda Stamps, October 26, 1992.

2. Sermon notes from personal files of Don Stamps.

3. Sermon notes from personal files of Don Stamps.

4. Linda Stamps interview.

5. Personal files of Don Stamps.

6. Interview with Loren Rovenstine, September 14, 1992.

7. Interview with Bob and Irma Silkman, September 8, 1992.

8. Linda Stamps interview and personal files of Don Stamps.

9. Undated letter from Wesley Adams to Don Stamps.

10. Sermon notes from files of Don Stamps.

CHAPTER 10

1. Interview with U.S. Grant, July 3, 1992.

2. Edith Waldvogel Blumhofer, *The Assemblies of God: A Popular History* (Springfield, Missouri, Gospel Publishing House, 1985), pp. 36-37.

3. William Menzies, *Anointed to Serve* (Springfield, Gospel Publishing House, 1971), Sections 7 and 8 in appendix.

4. Tape letter from Don Stamps to Wesley Adams, December, 1978.

5. Tape letter from Stamps to Adams.

6. Interview with Bobby Stamps, September 14, 1992.

7. Interview with Paul Lowenberg, September 8, 1992.

8. Interview with Derald Musgrove, September 8, 1992.

9. U.S. Grant interview.

10. Interview with Loren Triplett, October 31, 1992 and Linda Stamps, October 26, 1992.

11 Letter from Don Stamps to Dr. B. Edgar Johnson, April 3, 1979.

12. Paul Lowenberg interview.

13. Linda Stamps interview.

14. Interview with Gary Davidson, August 8, 1992.

15. Letter from Quinton McGhee to the author, October 1, 1992.

16. Gary Davidson interview.

17. Interview with Woody and Emma Stamps, September 2, 1992.

18. Ruth Tucker, *From Jerusalem to Irian Jaya* (Grand Rapids, Zondervan Publishing House, 1983), pp. 455-458.

19. Don Stamps, "Ten Days at Prayer Mountain Made the Difference," *Church Growth*, December, 1984, pp. 20-21.

20. Interview with Linda Stamps, August 12, 1992 and Don Stamps, p. 21 (see note 19).

CHAPTER 11

1. Brazil, "Field Focus," Division of Foreign Missions, The Assemblies of God, Springfield, Missouri, March, 1978.

2. "Evangel News Digest," Pentecostal Evangel, April 6, 1986, pp. 12-13.

3. "Field Focus" article (see number 1 above).

4. Letter from Don Stamps to Wesley Adams, June 8, 1981.

5. Tape letter from Don Stamps to Bob Silkman, March, 1982.

6. Interview of Linda Stamps with David A. Womack, 1994.

7. Interview with Linda Stamps.

8. Interview with Linda Stamps, October 26, 1992, and with Toby, Todd, and Tiffany Stamps, August 25, 1992.

9. Stamps to Silkman tape.

10. Letter from Don Stamps to Bob Silkman, May, 1982.

11. Stamps to Silkman tape.

12. Interview with Dave Harrison, October 15, 1992.

13. *Pentecostal Evangel* article. (see number 2 above).

14. Dave Harrison interview.

15. Dave Harrison interview.

16. Letter From Rick Hoover to author, December 2, 1992.

17. Personal files of Don and Linda Stamps.

CHAPTER 12

1. Interview with Gary Davidson, August 8, 1992 and Wesley Adams, September 18, 1992.

2. Ruth Tucker, "From Jerusalem to Irian Jaya" (Grand Rapids, Zondervan Publishing House, 1983), pp. 304-306.

3. Interview with Stanley Horton, September 4, 1992.

4. Gary Davidson interview.

5. Letter from Don Stamps to Loren Triplett, March 17, 1980.

6. "A Modern Man With a Mission," Research paper, Keisha Dunning Mind, Central Bible College, April 22, 1992.

7. Tape letter from Don Stamps to Bob Silkman, March, 1983.

8. Tape letter from Don Stamps to Bob Silkman, September, 1983.

9. Letter from Don Stamps to Wesley Adams, March 31, 1982.

10. Same as #9.

11. Interview with Wesley Adams, September 18, 1992.

12. *The Daily News*, Olathe, Kansas, March 12, 1983, p. 1.

13. Letter from Wesley Adams to Dr. Curtis Smith, March 4, 1983.

14. Interview with Stanley Horton, September 4, 1992.

15. Letter from William Menzies to author, October 1, 1992. *Anointed to Serve* (Gospel Publishing House, 1971) is an official history of the General Council of the Assemblies of God.

16. Letter from French Arrington to author, September 24, 1992.

17. Interview with Robert Shank, September 20, 1992.

18. Letter from Richard Waters to author, October 1, 1992.

19. Interview with Roy Winbush, September 16, 1992.

20. Letter from Roger Stronstad to Don Stamps, February 7, 1988.

21. October 1, 1992, Menzies to Burke letter.

22. Same as #21.

23. Interview with Verlyn Verbrugge, September 23, 1992.

24. Interview with Verbrugge.

25. Letter from David Wilkerson to Don Stamps, June 1, 1990.

26. Leonard Ravenhill letter in the files of Wesley Adams.

27. Letter from Don Stamps to Loren Triplett, July 15, 1990.

28. Preface to *The Full Life Study Bible* (New Testament) (Grand Rapids, Michigan, Zondervan Publishing House, 1990).

29. Interview with Loren Triplett, October 31, 1992.

30. Interview with Joseph W. Kilpatrick, April 8, 1993.

31. Interview with Charles Stewart, Life Publishers, March 23, 1993.

CHAPTER 13

1. Interview with Linda Stamps, October 26, 1992.

2. Interview with Ossie Jones, October 26, 1992.

3. Interview with Gary Davidson, August 8, 1992.

4. Ossie Jones interview.

5. Interview with Wesley Adams, September 18, 1992.

6. Wesley Adams interview, Gary Davidsion interview, and interview with Dave Harrison, October 15, 1992.

7. Interview with Lawrence Williams, September 8, 1992.

8. Sermon notes of Linda Stamps.

9. Ossie Jones interview.

10. Notes from *The Full Life Study Bible*.

11. Sermon notes of Linda Stamps.

12. Letter from Loren Triplett to Don Stamps, October 30, 1991.

13. Interview with Larry Fine, September 17, 1992.

14. Personal files of Don Stamps.

15. Linda Stamps interview.

16. Remarks made at Don Stamps' funeral, November 11, 1991.

17. Remarks made at funeral, November 11, 1991.

18. Remarks made at funeral, November 11, 1991.

19. Interview with David Fine, September 20, 1992.

20. Interview with U.S. Grant, July 3, 1992.

21. Interview with Stanley Horton, September 4, 1992.

22. Ossie Jones interview.

23. Loren Triplett interview.

CHAPTER 14

1. Interview with Loren Triplett, October 31, 1992.

2. Personal files of Don Stamps.

3. Personal files of Don Stamps.

4. Interview with Gary Davidson, August 8, 1992.

5. Interview with Dave Harrison, October 15, 1992.

6. Interview with Stanley Horton, September 4, 1992.

7. Letter from William Menzies to author, October 1, 1992.

8. Letter from Rick Hoover to author, December 2, 1992.

9. Interview with Joseph W. Kilpatrick, April 8, 1993.

10. *The Full Life Study Bible*, Zondervan Publishing House, Grand Rapids, Michigan, (NIV), 1992, p. 1898.

11. *FLSB*, p. 1882-83.

12. *FLSB*, p. 1854.

13. Tape letter from Don Stamps to Wesley Adams, July, 1982.

14. *FLSB*, p. 1395.

15. *FLSB*, p. 1654.

16. *FLSB*, p. 1646.

17. Sermon notes in personal files of Don Stamps.

18. Sermon of Don Stamps at Central Bible College, November 14, 1990.

A Tribute from J. Wesley Adams

A DILIGENT MAN OF PRAYER

I am grateful, and will be eternally, for my thirty-year friendship with Don Stamps. He was in every respect an unusual individualist, as unconventional as an Old Testament prophet and as intensely serious about the gospel as a New Testament apostle.

I first met Don in 1961-62 at Bethany Nazarene College, Bethany, Oklahoma, where we were both theological students preparing for the ministry. He was the student grader for my Greek professor, and we became acquainted through my Greek exams. Besides having the same college major and course of studies, we both had handicaps that were a major challenge to our entering the full-time ministry. At our college commencement in May, 1964, Don pushed me in my manual wheelchair from the auditorium during the recessional march. For us it was the commencement of a life-long friendship and partnership in the work of the gospel.

Don was a man with a brilliant intellect, a razor-sharp analytical mind, a tenacious and strong will, an adventuresome spirit, and a strength and intensity of personality that combined together to make him an intimidating person for those who did not know him well. But for those who really knew Don, he was a warm-hearted, stimulating, and generous individual. He was as dedicated a father as I have ever seen and the most loyal friend a man could have. It was nothing for him to drive 400 or 500 miles to visit a friend for two days. To be his friend was to be challenged constantly to think clearly about the great and important issues of life.

One supremely important issue for Don was God's Word. He had a high view of the Bible as the inerrant and infallible Word of God. For him it was the plumbline of truth by which all of life was to be measured.

Also, Don took seriously the cost of discipleship as set forth by Jesus. He believed strongly that the price tag of discipleship included the cross and bearing the sufferings of Christ. He knew from Scripture and personal experience that God's calling always involves blessing and suffering, joy and sorrow, successes and disappointments.

Few men have grappled as intently as Don with the biblical meaning of sanctification and its practical implications for the true believer. After years of studying the Scriptures and reflecting on this issue, he strongly believed that the true nature of God's saving grace was to teach us "to deny ungodliness and worldly desires and to live sensibly, righteously and godly in the present age, looking for the blessed hope" of Christ's return (Titus 2:12-13a). For Don, God's redemptive purpose in Christ was not only to forgive our sins (regeneration) but also to deliver us from all unrighteousness (sanctification). This Biblical truth is proclaimed by Don throughout the pages of *The Full Life Study Bible*.

Like Jesus, Don was a man who loved righteousness and hated evil (Heb. 1:9). Many good men have demonstrated one or the other of these two virtues; Don embodied them both in tension and intensity. He had little tolerance for ministers who compromised or watered down the gospel in order to make it more palatable to our generation.

As a Spirit-filled theologian, Don weighed carefully the essential meaning of the kingdom of God as proclaimed by Jesus and the early church. He profoundly understood that its proclamation involved confrontation with and the plunder of Satan's kingdom as the god of this age. He knew that only the supernatural power of the Holy Spirit could enable that proclamation to go forth today and make a difference in our world.

Don was a devoted and disciplined man of prayer. He demonstrated in his life the apostolic priority of Peter and the Twelve whose calling was to devote themselves to prayer and the ministry of the Word (Acts 6:4). Whereas a typical seminary student spends 10 minutes or less a day in prayer, Don spent one to two hours daily as a result of his intense desire for communion with God. He faithfully kept his commitment to God of two hours a day in prayer and the devotional study of the Word throughout his ministry in Brazil. His love for the Lord Jesus and God's Word remained strong, fervent, and intense because of his disciplined prayer-life.

As Don diligently and fervently pursued God, God took him through some crushing experiences. As the full fragrance of a rose petal is not released until it is crushed, so God's grace in Don's life was not fully released to affect others until he had gone through some crushing experiences. Ultimately Don's strong will and independent spirit was broken by God, making him fully usable as a vessel for honor. The depth of his life in God enabled him to do great things for God in the life span of only fifty-three years.

While writing this tribute to my close friend on the last day of 1992 and anticipating the purposes of God that are yet ahead, I am reminded again of how adventuresome a man Don was. He was always pressing on to what was ahead, rather than looking back or holding on to something in the past. On November 7, 1991, only a few weeks after completing all notes for *The Full Life Study Bible*, Don pressed on to the ultimate and eternal goal of being with the Lord. As you followed his life's journey through the pages of this book, from his chaotic youth (before conversion) to his writing the study Bible, I pray his unique life as redeemed by Christ will profoundly impact you as it has me and others who knew him.

— J. Wesley Adams
Author of the Bible book introductions for
The Full Life Study Bible

Don Stamps, My Friend

My friend...yes, he was my friend
but more.

Sounding board...confidant...
counselor...kindred spirit...

Opinionated, yet most of the time
sure of those opinions.

Loud with his views, death on sin
and depravity.

Loved his family mountains...
agape cared for them.

He had his own inimitable way with words
and thoughts and ideas.
He expressed himself
rather clearly, bluntly
about the truth.

Push Back the Darkness

He tenaciously pursued righteousness
    and seethed over the wickedness
      of the wicked.

Inquisitive...definitely ambitious
    with regards to spiritual issues...
    defender of Gospel purity.

He would challenge your theology,
    temper test your doctrinal ideologies
    and often bow your head
    with his honed and hallmark convictions.

We had our times; sometimes majestic,
    sometimes sobering,
    sometimes I wanted to clobber him.

He finished his race,
    ran it like a conquering warrior,
    snapping the finish line tape
    weak, stumbling, emaciated in body,
    but gloriously triumphant in spirit.

I miss him...I miss him a lot.
    One day, though, I am going
    to see him again.
Times are going to be wonderful again.

— Missionary Rick Hoover
Brazil

The Truth about Television, by Donald C. Stamps

In his ministry in Brazil, Don Stamps traveled among the Assemblies of God churches and often gave his presentation on the problems with television. Brazilian Christians do not watch television because what it depicts so often runs contrary to Christian standards. The following article came from his experience of speaking on this important subject. Whereas he used the New American Standard Bible to write his study notes, in this particular case he used the New International Version.

Does the same teaching apply to America and other countries? We can only say that many of the same reasons Don Stamps had for opposing it in Brazil are now present around the world.

— **Bob Burke and David A. Womack**

THE TRUTH ABOUT TELEVISION, BY DONALD C. STAMPS

Satan is using the images and memories of television to lead us astray. Jesus said, "If the world hates you, keep in mind that it hated me first" (John 15:18, NIV). Satan is the prince of this earth. The things of this world, including television, are hostile to God. Satan is using television against Christ. As the end of time approaches, he will use it more and more against the laws, the morality, and the ways of God. He will do this to destroy the work of God, the church, His people, and Christian families. Secular television is the greatest threat to the salvation of your children. Television exposes our minds to a world that simply ignores God.

The average teenager watches 18,000 murders and thousands of rapes, machine gunnings, bombings, and other acts of violence on television. A recent survey of 400 television programs found 310 murders, 180 lies, 165 robberies, and more than 200 acts of adultery. This is called entertainment. It is actually death, destruction, and sexual infidelity. These have become our chief form of entertainment. Have we gone so far that death, cruelty, and immorality are also entertainment for Christians?

Television glorifies godless heroes and evil people. God is mocked. Biblical commandments are laughed at. Television does not honor God. It professes to be the wisdom of this age. It has rejected God. It says pleasure can only be found in lust and impurity. It teaches that homosexuality is not a sin. It appeals to the degraded passions of both men and women. It does not acknowledge God as Creator and Lord of the universe. It teaches there is no absolute right or wrong.

I know that all television is not evil. Satan is no fool. If television were 100-percent evil, Christians would not be so easily deceived. If Satan can place good programs along with the bad, he wins. If sixty percent of television programs are good, the forty percent of evil programming will be sufficient to undermine the spirituality of God's people.

What is television doing to the church? It is destroying the grace of God in our lives. Grace is the God-given desire and power to do the will of God. It is the hunger and thirst for the things of God. If that hunger is choked by television, a Christian cannot fulfill God's purpose in his life. For example, the Holy Spirit may tell you to pray and read your Bible; but instead you watch television for two or three hours and find you no longer want to pray or read the Word. The desire has been choked. The more we watch television, the more our hunger and thirst for the things of God will diminish.

Television shapes the way of looking at the world. It fashions our whole way of thinking. It causes moral confusion. It weakens convictions. It breaks down resistance to temptation and makes it easier to sin. Whatever evil you visualize becomes easier to commit. Watching an act on television breaks down the resistance to a specific temptation. When we are watching television, we are participating in what is going on. We are not just passive watchers. What is on the screen is really going on in our minds. Television dramas stir our emotions. We cry and laugh with the actors. As we watch evil, we experience evil, and any evil experienced is easier to do the second time. Remember that your body is the temple of the Holy Spirit. We are not to put these evil imaginations in our heart.

The violence on television desensitizes both children and adults to human suffering. Screams of pain and murder no longer hurt us. We can actually yawn while we are watching it. After a while, there is no feeling for human misery and suffering or even death. We are warned that because iniquity abounds, the love of many will wax cold.

Television is causing the decay of biblical sexual morality. Satan, through television, has launched an attack against the standards of morality and decency. Ungodly ethics are sent into our homes in almost every television drama in the form of humor and entertainment. The motive of Satan is to change our traditional values of Christian morality. This kind of deception should make us angry. We should be zealous for our God and for His standards. If you let your child watch the average television program, do not be surprised if you find him eventually engaged in immorality, in sexual sins, and in deep trouble spiritually.

Today's television is giving our children ungodly heroes. It encourages them to be like godless men and women if they want to be popular and successful. Television teaches our children to be cynical of all people, especially parents, pastors, and public officers. The children are taught to "do their own thing," to be absolutely independent. This leads to rebellion against all authority. Allowing our children to watch television makes it difficult for the church to teach them to remain separated from the world. They naturally want the joys and pleasures they see in the lives portrayed on television.

We are humans and are subject to the desires of this world. The Bible tells us that every man is tempted when he is drawn away of his own lust. If you enjoy moral impurity on television, here is what happens to you:

1. Impurity destroys the work of the Holy Spirit in your life.(Gal. 5:17)

2. Impurity destroys your love toward God and your family.(Matt. 24:12)

3. Impurity destroys your ability to give effective discipline. (Prov. 22:8—"He who sows wickedness reaps trouble, and the rod of his fury will be destroyed" (kalah, utterly destroyed).

4. Impurity destroys your sensitivity to the real needs of your family.

You cannot love the immorality on television and love God. "If any man loves the world, the love of the father is not in him." (1 John 2:15)

What effect should television have on Christians?

1. We should be grieved and saddened as is the Holy Spirit for the sin of this generation.

2. We should be angry...angry at the sin and angry at the hurt that television is doing to our God and His church. We should be jealous for our God.

3. We should weep because of the millions of souls being deceived and tempted, on their way to hell because of the influence of television. We should be like Jeremiah who wept for the sins of his people.

4. We should purpose in our hearts to fight and hate evil more than ever before. When we see the scourge of destruction and brokenness in human lives caused by the immorality of television, we should determine to love righteousness and hate evil.

We know that the origin of secular television is Satan. It is Satan who is putting the temptation before us, our families, and our children. God has given us clear steps of action on how to resist the devil so that he will flee from us. James 4:6-10 says, "But he gives us more grace. That is why

Scripture says: 'God opposes the proud but gives grace to the humble.' Submit yourselves, then, to God. Resist the devil, and he will flee from you. Come near to God and he will come near to you. Wash your hands, you sinners, and purify your hearts, you double-minded. Grieve, mourn and wail. Change your laughter to mourning and your joy to gloom. Humble yourselves before the Lord, and he will lift you up."

If you have allowed sin, through television, to dominate your life, here is what you need to do:

1. Use the power of God to overcome the allure of secular television in your life. Claim the promise that sin cannot have dominion over you because greater is He that is in you than he that is in the world.

2. Get more grace. You cannot conquer temptation with your own willpower. God must give you the desire and the power to do his will.

3. Submit to God. You cannot be your own boss. You must submit to God's Word and obey the promptings of the Holy Spirit.

4. Recognize that the violence, the sex, the hatred, and the worldly philosophies are from Satan. Ask God to rebuke Satan in the name of and through the blood of Jesus Christ. Learn scriptures that relate directly to the temptation.

5. Draw near to God.

6. Cleanse your hands. Satan will cause you to remember the terrible things you have already seen on television. Confess, in the presence of God, and ask Him to forgive you for allowing Satan to place the mental images in your mind. When you cleanse your conscience, your mind will be given new power over temptation.

7. Memorize James 4:4. "You adulterous people, don't you know that friendship with the world is hatred toward God? Anyone who chooses to be a friend of the world becomes an enemy of God."

For the church, secular television is a life-or-death situation. If we let down our guard, the church will be infiltrated by worldliness, wrong philosophies, evil desires, and compromise. The church will lose the power given to it by the Holy Spirit to take the gospel to the four corners of the earth.